Microsoft Teams
Complete Self-Assessment Guide

The guidance in this Self-Assessment is based on Microsoft Teams best practices and standards in business process architecture, design and quality management. The guidance is also based on the professional judgment of the individual collaborators listed in the Acknowledgments.

Notice of rights

The information in this book is distributed on an "As Is" basis without warranty. While every precaution has been taken in the preparation of he book, neither the author nor the publisher shall have any liability to any person or entity with respect to any loss or damage caused or alleged to be caused directly or indirectly by the instructions contained in this book or by the products described in it.

Trademarks

Many of the designations used by manufacturers and sellers to distinguish their products are claimed as trademarks. Where those designations appear in this book, and the publisher was aware of a trademark claim, the designations appear as requested by the owner of the trademark. All other product names and services identified throughout this book are used in editorial fashion only and for the benefit of such companies with no intention of infringement of the trademark. No such use, or the use of any trade name, is intended to convey endorsement or other affiliation with this book.

Table of Contents

About The Art of Service

The Art of Service, Business Process Architects since 2000, is dedicated to helping stakeholders achieve excellence.

Defining, designing, creating, and implementing a process to solve a stakeholders challenge or meet an objective is the most valuable role… In EVERY group, company, organization and department.

Unless you're talking a one-time, single-use project, there should be a process. Whether that process is managed and implemented by humans, AI, or a combination of the two, it needs to be designed by someone with a complex enough perspective to ask the right questions.

Someone capable of asking the right questions and step back and say, 'What are we really trying to accomplish here? And is there a different way to look at it?'

With The Art of Service's Standard Requirements Self-Assessments, we empower people who can do just that — whether their title is marketer, entrepreneur, manager, salesperson, consultant, Business Process Manager, executive assistant, IT Manager, CIO etc... —they are the people who rule the future. They are people who watch the process as it happens, and ask the right questions to make the process work better.

Contact us when you need any support with this Self-Assessment and any help with templates, blue-prints and examples of standard documents you might need:

http://theartofservice.com
service@theartofservice.com

Acknowledgments

This checklist was developed under the auspices of The Art of Service, chaired by Gerardus Blokdyk.

Representatives from several client companies participated in the preparation of this Self-Assessment.

In addition, we are thankful for the design and printing services provided.

Included Resources - how to access

Included with your purchase of the book is the Microsoft Teams Self-Assessment Spreadsheet Dashboard which contains all questions and Self-Assessment areas and auto-generates insights, graphs, and project RACI planning - all with examples to get you started right away.

How? Simply send an email to
access@theartofservice.com
with this books' title in the subject to get the Microsoft Teams Self Assessment Tool right away.

You will receive the following contents with New and Updated specific criteria:

- The latest quick edition of the book in PDF

- The latest complete edition of the book in PDF, which criteria correspond to the criteria in...

- The Self-Assessment Excel Dashboard, and...

- Example pre-filled Self-Assessment Excel Dashboard to get familiar with results generation

- In-depth specific Checklists covering the topic

- Project management checklists and templates to assist with implementation

INCLUDES LIFETIME SELF ASSESSMENT UPDATES

Every self assessment comes with Lifetime Updates and Lifetime Free Updated Books. Lifetime Updates is an industry-first feature which allows you to receive verified self assessment updates, ensuring you always have the most accurate information at your fingertips.

Get it now- you will be glad you did - do it now, before you forget.

Send an email to **access@theartofservice.com** with this books' title in the subject to get the Microsoft Teams Self Assessment Tool right away.

Your feedback is invaluable to us

If you recently bought this book, we would love to hear from you! You can do this by writing a review on amazon (or the online store where you purchased this book) about your last purchase! As part of our continual service improvement process, we love to hear real client experiences and feedback.

How does it work?
To post a review on Amazon, just log in to your account and click on the Create Your Own Review button (under Customer Reviews) of the relevant product page. You can find examples of product reviews in Amazon. If you purchased from another online store, simply follow their procedures.

What happens when I submit my review?
Once you have submitted your review, send us an email at review@theartofservice.com with the link to your review so we can properly thank you for your feedback.

Purpose of this Self-Assessment

This Self-Assessment has been developed to improve understanding of the requirements and elements of Microsoft Teams, based on best practices and standards in business process architecture, design and quality management.

It is designed to allow for a rapid Self-Assessment to determine how closely existing management practices and procedures correspond to the elements of the Self-Assessment.

The criteria of requirements and elements of Microsoft Teams have been rephrased in the format of a Self-Assessment questionnaire, with a seven-criterion scoring system, as explained in this document.

In this format, even with limited background knowledge

of Microsoft Teams, a manager can quickly review existing operations to determine how they measure up to the standards. This in turn can serve as the starting point of a 'gap analysis' to identify management tools or system elements that might usefully be implemented in the organization to help improve overall performance.

How to use the Self-Assessment

On the following pages are a series of questions to identify to what extent your Microsoft Teams initiative is complete in comparison to the requirements set in standards.

To facilitate answering the questions, there is a space in front of each question to enter a score on a scale of '1' to '5'.

1 Strongly Disagree

2 Disagree

3 Neutral

4 Agree

5 Strongly Agree

Read the question and rate it with the following in front of mind:

'In my belief,
the answer to this question is clearly defined'.

There are two ways in which you can choose to interpret this statement;
1. how aware are you that the answer to the question is clearly defined
2. for more in-depth analysis you can choose to gather

evidence and confirm the answer to the question. This obviously will take more time, most Self-Assessment users opt for the first way to interpret the question and dig deeper later on based on the outcome of the overall Self-Assessment.

A score of '1' would mean that the answer is not clear at all, where a '5' would mean the answer is crystal clear and defined. Leave emtpy when the question is not applicable or you don't want to answer it, you can skip it without affecting your score. Write your score in the space provided.

After you have responded to all the appropriate statements in each section, compute your average score for that section, using the formula provided, and round to the nearest tenth. Then transfer to the corresponding spoke in the Microsoft Teams Scorecard on the second next page of the Self-Assessment.

Your completed Microsoft Teams Scorecard will give you a clear presentation of which Microsoft Teams areas need attention.

Microsoft Teams
Scorecard Example

Example of how the finalized Scorecard can look like:

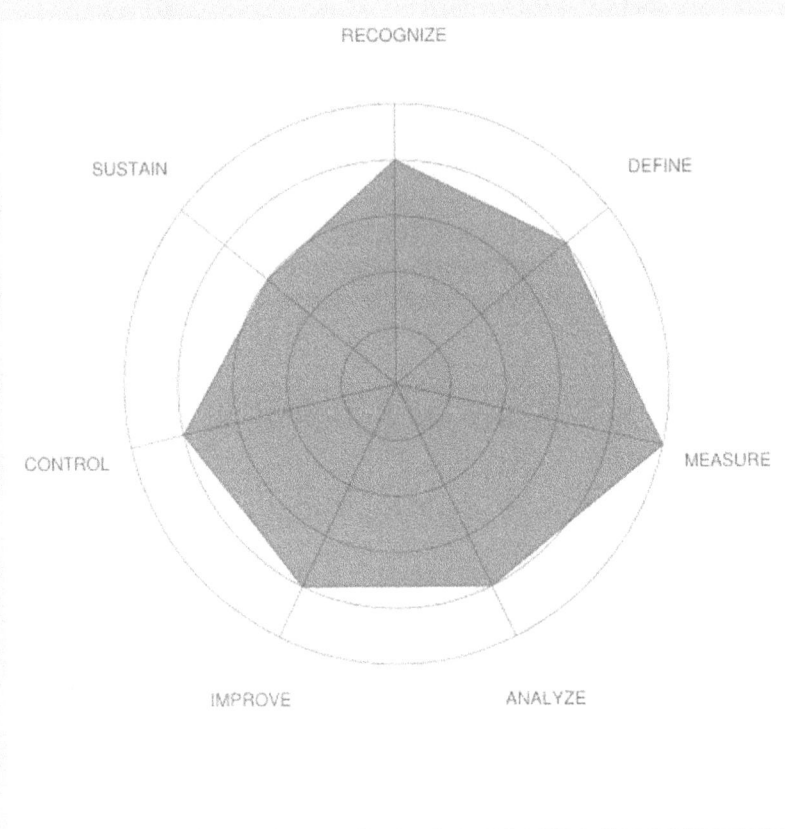

Microsoft Teams Scorecard

Your Scores:

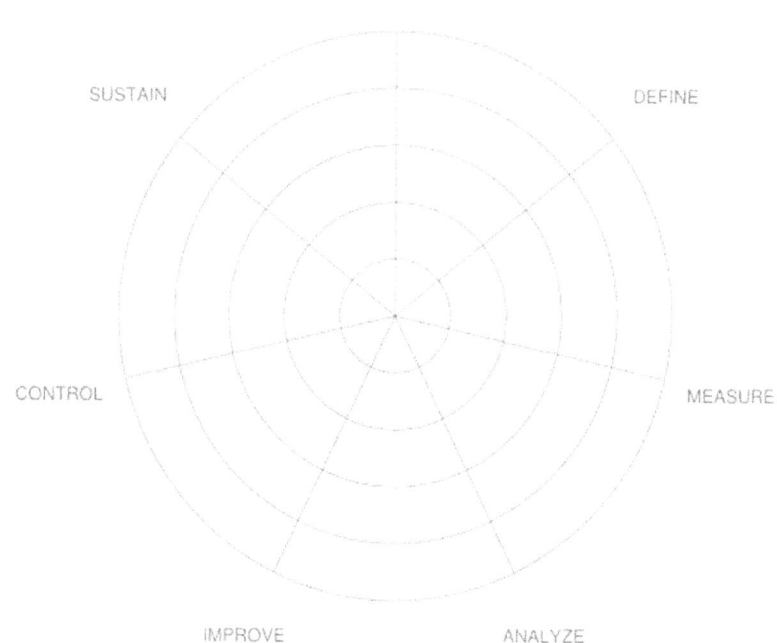

BEGINNING OF THE SELF-ASSESSMENT:

CRITERION #1: RECOGNIZE

INTENT: Be aware of the need for change. Recognize that there is an unfavorable variation, problem or symptom.

In my belief, the answer to this question is clearly defined:

5 Strongly Agree

4 Agree

3 Neutral

2 Disagree

1 Strongly Disagree

1. For your Microsoft Teams project, identify and describe the business environment, is there more than one layer to the business environment?
<--- Score

2. Who needs to know about Microsoft Teams?
<--- Score

3. Do you need to avoid or amend any Microsoft

Teams activities?
<--- Score

4. As a sponsor, customer or management, how important is it to meet goals, objectives?
<--- Score

5. What needs to be done?
<--- Score

6. What do I need to do specifically in my cloud application so that it can restore itself back to original state in an event of failure (hardware or software)?
<--- Score

7. What training and capacity building actions are needed to implement proposed reforms?
<--- Score

8. Will a response program recognize when a crisis occurs and provide some level of response?
<--- Score

9. Are employees recognized or rewarded for performance that demonstrates the highest levels of integrity?
<--- Score

10. Will it solve real problems?
<--- Score

11. What does Microsoft Teams success mean to the stakeholders?
<--- Score

12. Looking at each person individually – does every one have the qualities which are needed to work in this group?
<--- Score

13. Can management personnel recognize the monetary benefit of Microsoft Teams?
<--- Score

14. Is the need for organizational change recognized?
<--- Score

15. What are the existing research issues and what should be the future research agenda in legacy to cloud migration?
<--- Score

16. Should you invest in industry-recognized qualications?
<--- Score

17. Are there recognized Microsoft Teams problems?
<--- Score

18. What are the minority interests and what amount of minority interests can be recognized?
<--- Score

19. Who needs what information?
<--- Score

20. How does it fit into your organizational needs and tasks?
<--- Score

21. Will Microsoft Teams deliverables need to be

tested and, if so, by whom?
<--- Score

22. What tools and technologies are needed for a custom Microsoft Teams project?
<--- Score

23. When a Microsoft Teams manager recognizes a problem, what options are available?
<--- Score

24. Do you need different information or graphics?
<--- Score

25. To what extent would your organization benefit from being recognized as a award recipient?
<--- Score

26. Required Skills: Who Do We Need?
<--- Score

27. The foundation for a successful acquisition consists of clear answers to three questions: what do I need, when do I need it, and how do I know its good when I get it?
<--- Score

28. How much are sponsors, customers, partners, stakeholders involved in Microsoft Teams? In other words, what are the risks, if Microsoft Teams does not deliver successfully?
<--- Score

29. What problems are you facing and how do you consider Microsoft Teams will circumvent those obstacles?

<--- Score

30. Does Microsoft Teams create potential expectations in other areas that need to be recognized and considered?
<--- Score

31. Does your organization need more Microsoft Teams education?
<--- Score

32. Who had the original idea?
<--- Score

33. Are you dealing with any of the same issues today as yesterday? What can you do about this?
<--- Score

34. What prevents you from making the changes you know will make you a more effective Microsoft Teams leader?
<--- Score

35. What are your needs in relation to Microsoft Teams skills, labor, equipment, and markets?
<--- Score

36. How are the Microsoft Teams's objectives aligned to the organization's overall business strategy?
<--- Score

37. What information do users need?
<--- Score

38. Consider your own Microsoft Teams project, what types of organizational problems do you think might

be causing or affecting your problem, based on the work done so far?
<--- Score

39. What else needs to be measured?
<--- Score

40. Will new equipment/products be required to facilitate Microsoft Teams delivery, for example is new software needed?
<--- Score

41. Do you have/need 24-hour access to key personnel?
<--- Score

42. What would happen if Microsoft Teams weren't done?
<--- Score

43. Are there Microsoft Teams problems defined?
<--- Score

44. Are controls defined to recognize and contain problems?
<--- Score

45. What are the expected benefits of Microsoft Teams to the business?
<--- Score

46. Think about the people you identified for your Microsoft Teams project and the project responsibilities you would assign to them. what kind of training do you think they would need to perform these responsibilities effectively?

<--- Score

47. Are your goals realistic? Do you need to redefine your problem? Perhaps the problem has changed or maybe you have reached your goal and need to set a new one?
<--- Score

48. What is the problem or issue?
<--- Score

49. How do you identify the kinds of information that you will need?
<--- Score

50. Are problem definition and motivation clearly presented?
<--- Score

51. Who are your key stakeholders who need to sign off?
<--- Score

52. Is it clear when you think of the day ahead of you what activities and tasks you need to complete?
<--- Score

53. What do you need to start doing?
<--- Score

54. To what extent does each concerned units management team recognize Microsoft Teams as an effective investment?
<--- Score

55. What are the business objectives to be achieved

with Microsoft Teams?

<--- Score

56. What extra resources will you need?

<--- Score

57. What vendors make products that address the Microsoft Teams needs?

<--- Score

58. What should be considered when identifying available resources, constraints, and deadlines?

<--- Score

59. What are the timeframes required to resolve each of the issues/problems?

<--- Score

60. Who defines the rules in relation to any given issue?

<--- Score

61. How do you assess your Microsoft Teams workforce capability and capacity needs, including skills, competencies, and staffing levels?

<--- Score

62. What situation(s) led to this Microsoft Teams Self Assessment?

<--- Score

63. Do you know what you need to know about Microsoft Teams?

<--- Score

64. Are there any specific expectations or concerns

about the Microsoft Teams team, Microsoft Teams itself?
<--- Score

65. Are there any revenue recognition issues?
<--- Score

66. Who else hopes to benefit from it?
<--- Score

67. How can auditing be a preventative security measure?
<--- Score

68. How are you going to measure success?
<--- Score

69. How do you take a forward-looking perspective in identifying Microsoft Teams research related to market response and models?
<--- Score

70. What is the smallest subset of the problem you can usefully solve?
<--- Score

Add up total points for this section:

_ _ _ _ _ = Total points for this section

Divided by: _ _ _ _ _ _ (number of statements answered) = _ _ _ _ _ _
Average score for this section

Transfer your score to the Microsoft Teams Index at the beginning of the Self-Assessment.

CRITERION #2: DEFINE:

INTENT: Formulate the business problem. Define the problem, needs and objectives.

In my belief, the answer to this question is clearly defined:

5 Strongly Agree

4 Agree

3 Neutral

2 Disagree

1 Strongly Disagree

1. How is the team tracking and documenting its work?
<--- Score

2. Are resource requirements stable and well within the provisions of cloud provider selected?
<--- Score

3. Has your scope been defined?

<--- Score

4. Is Microsoft Teams currently on schedule according to the plan?
<--- Score

5. Are there different segments of customers?
<--- Score

6. Is there a completed SIPOC representation, describing the Suppliers, Inputs, Process, Outputs, and Customers?
<--- Score

7. Is it clearly defined in and to your organization what you do?
<--- Score

8. Are improvement team members fully trained on Microsoft Teams?
<--- Score

9. What is out-of-scope initially?
<--- Score

10. Is the improvement team aware of the different versions of a process: what they think it is vs. what it actually is vs. what it should be vs. what it could be?
<--- Score

11. Is the current 'as is' process being followed? If not, what are the discrepancies?
<--- Score

12. Is the team sponsored by a champion or business leader?

<--- Score

13. Are there any constraints known that bear on the ability to perform Microsoft Teams work? How is the team addressing them?
<--- Score

14. Have specific policy objectives been defined?
<--- Score

15. Are audit criteria, scope, frequency and methods defined?
<--- Score

16. What is the scope of the Microsoft Teams effort?
<--- Score

17. Do I have the necessary cloud-aware system administration tools required to manage and maintain my applications?
<--- Score

18. What key business process output measure(s) does Microsoft Teams leverage and how?
<--- Score

19. What is the scope of Microsoft Teams?
<--- Score

20. Does the team have regular meetings?
<--- Score

21. Who defines (or who defined) the rules and roles?
<--- Score

22. Are different versions of process maps needed to

account for the different types of inputs?
<--- Score

23. Does the scope remain the same?
<--- Score

24. Have the customer needs been translated into specific, measurable requirements? How?
<--- Score

25. How does the Microsoft Teams manager ensure against scope creep?
<--- Score

26. Does the cloud provide all of the infrastructure building blocks we require?
<--- Score

27. If substitutes have been appointed, have they been briefed on the Microsoft Teams goals and received regular communications as to the progress to date?
<--- Score

28. Will team members regularly document their Microsoft Teams work?
<--- Score

29. Are required metrics defined, what are they?
<--- Score

30. Is there a completed, verified, and validated high-level 'as is' (not 'should be' or 'could be') business process map?
<--- Score

31. Has/have the customer(s) been identified?
<--- Score

32. What are the rough order estimates on cost savings/opportunities that Microsoft Teams brings?
<--- Score

33. Will team members perform Microsoft Teams work when assigned and in a timely fashion?
<--- Score

34. Do you all define Microsoft Teams in the same way?
<--- Score

35. Has the improvement team collected the 'voice of the customer' (obtained feedback – qualitative and quantitative)?
<--- Score

36. Is scope creep really all bad news?
<--- Score

37. What are the boundaries of the scope? What is in bounds and what is not? What is the start point? What is the stop point?
<--- Score

38. What are the dynamics of the communication plan?
<--- Score

39. Have all of the relationships been defined properly?
<--- Score

40. How do you keep key subject matter experts in the loop?
<--- Score

41. What system do you use for gathering Microsoft Teams information?
<--- Score

42. Has the direction changed at all during the course of Microsoft Teams? If so, when did it change and why?
<--- Score

43. Has everyone on the team, including the team leaders, been properly trained?
<--- Score

44. Has a project plan, Gantt chart, or similar been developed/completed?
<--- Score

45. How do you manage scope?
<--- Score

46. What is out of scope?
<--- Score

47. What are the tasks and definitions?
<--- Score

48. How much effort (in terms of building new or modifying existing tools) is required to move the application?
<--- Score

49. How can the value of Microsoft Teams be defined?

<--- Score

50. How did the Microsoft Teams manager receive input to the development of a Microsoft Teams improvement plan and the estimated completion dates/times of each activity?
<--- Score

51. Are accountability and ownership for Microsoft Teams clearly defined?
<--- Score

52. What specifically is the problem? Where does it occur? When does it occur? What is its extent?
<--- Score

53. Have all basic functions of Microsoft Teams been defined?
<--- Score

54. Does the cloud support the identity and authentication mechanism you require?
<--- Score

55. Are approval levels defined for contracts and supplements to contracts?
<--- Score

56. Are resource requirements of application stable and well within the offerings of the cloud provider?
<--- Score

57. When was the Microsoft Teams start date?
<--- Score

58. What constraints exist that might impact the team?
<--- Score

59. Are customer(s) identified and segmented according to their different needs and requirements?
<--- Score

60. Are resources adequate for the scope?
<--- Score

61. Is the team equipped with available and reliable resources?
<--- Score

62. Who are the Microsoft Teams improvement team members, including Management Leads and Coaches?
<--- Score

63. Is there a critical path to deliver Microsoft Teams results?
<--- Score

64. Is the Microsoft Teams scope complete and appropriately sized?
<--- Score

65. When are meeting minutes sent out? Who is on the distribution list?
<--- Score

66. What happens if Microsoft Teams's scope changes?
<--- Score

67. Is the team adequately staffed with the desired

cross-functionality? If not, what additional resources are available to the team?
<--- Score

68. What is in the scope and what is not in scope?
<--- Score

69. What scope to assess?
<--- Score

70. Is the team formed and are team leaders (Coaches and Management Leads) assigned?
<--- Score

71. Has the Microsoft Teams work been fairly and/or equitably divided and delegated among team members who are qualified and capable to perform the work? Has everyone contributed?
<--- Score

72. Is the scope of Microsoft Teams defined?
<--- Score

73. Is there a Microsoft Teams management charter, including business case, problem and goal statements, scope, milestones, roles and responsibilities, communication plan?
<--- Score

74. Is there regularly 100% attendance at the team meetings? If not, have appointed substitutes attended to preserve cross-functionality and full representation?
<--- Score

75. What is the context?

<--- Score

76. How will variation in the actual durations of each activity be dealt with to ensure that the expected Microsoft Teams results are met?
<--- Score

77. Is the Microsoft Teams scope manageable?
<--- Score

78. Is Microsoft Teams required?
<--- Score

79. Are business processes mapped?
<--- Score

80. What critical content must be communicated – who, what, when, where, and how?
<--- Score

81. Is Microsoft Teams linked to key business goals and objectives?
<--- Score

82. Are team charters developed?
<--- Score

83. Who is gathering Microsoft Teams information?
<--- Score

84. What is the definition of success?
<--- Score

85. Do the problem and goal statements meet the SMART criteria (specific, measurable, attainable, relevant, and time-bound)?

<--- Score

86. Are task requirements clearly defined?
<--- Score

87. What baselines are required to be defined and managed?
<--- Score

88. What are the Roles and Responsibilities for each team member and its leadership? Where is this documented?
<--- Score

89. What Microsoft Teams requirements should be gathered?
<--- Score

90. How was the 'as is' process map developed, reviewed, verified and validated?
<--- Score

91. What defines best in class?
<--- Score

92. If youre migrating applications to the cloud, do you know what your bandwidth requirements will be?
<--- Score

93. What customer feedback methods were used to solicit their input?
<--- Score

94. How do you hand over Microsoft Teams context?
<--- Score

95. What are the record-keeping requirements of Microsoft Teams activities?
<--- Score

96. What is the scope?
<--- Score

97. Is full participation by members in regularly held team meetings guaranteed?
<--- Score

98. When is the estimated completion date?
<--- Score

99. Are roles and responsibilities formally defined?
<--- Score

100. Has anyone else (internal or external to the organization) attempted to solve this problem or a similar one before? If so, what knowledge can be leveraged from these previous efforts?
<--- Score

101. What are the compelling business reasons for embarking on Microsoft Teams?
<--- Score

102. What was the context?
<--- Score

103. How and when will the baselines be defined?
<--- Score

104. What are the latency and bandwidth requirements?

<--- Score

105. Why are you doing Microsoft Teams and what is the scope?
<--- Score

106. What is in scope?
<--- Score

107. Scope of sensitive information?
<--- Score

108. How will the Microsoft Teams team and the organization measure complete success of Microsoft Teams?
<--- Score

109. In what way can you redefine the criteria of choice clients have in your category in your favor?
<--- Score

110. Is the application still being defined?
<--- Score

111. How would you define the culture at your organization, how susceptible is it to Microsoft Teams changes?
<--- Score

112. What sources do you use to gather information for a Microsoft Teams study?
<--- Score

113. Is data collected and displayed to better understand customer(s) critical needs and requirements.

<--- Score

114. How often are the team meetings?
<--- Score

115. Are customers identified and high impact areas defined?
<--- Score

116. How do you think the partners involved in Microsoft Teams would have defined success?
<--- Score

117. How do you gather Microsoft Teams requirements?
<--- Score

118. What would be the goal or target for a Microsoft Teams's improvement team?
<--- Score

119. Has a team charter been developed and communicated?
<--- Score

120. Has a high-level 'as is' process map been completed, verified and validated?
<--- Score

121. Is a fully trained team formed, supported, and committed to work on the Microsoft Teams improvements?
<--- Score

Add up total points for this section:
_ _ _ _ _ = Total points for this section

Divided by: _____ (number of
statements answered) = _____
Average score for this section

Transfer your score to the Microsoft
Teams Index at the beginning of the
Self-Assessment.

CRITERION #3: MEASURE:

INTENT: Gather the correct data.
Measure the current performance and
evolution of the situation.

In my belief, the answer to this
question is clearly defined:

5 Strongly Agree

4 Agree

3 Neutral

2 Disagree

1 Strongly Disagree

1. Does the Microsoft Teams task fit the client's priorities?
<--- Score

2. Have you found any 'ground fruit' or 'low-hanging fruit' for immediate remedies to the gap in performance?
<--- Score

3. Which measures and indicators matter?
<--- Score

4. How do your measurements capture actionable Microsoft Teams information for use in exceeding your customers expectations and securing your customers engagement?
<--- Score

5. What charts has the team used to display the components of variation in the process?
<--- Score

6. Is data collected on key measures that were identified?
<--- Score

7. Does Microsoft Teams analysis isolate the fundamental causes of problems?
<--- Score

8. What relevant entities could be measured?
<--- Score

9. How do you focus on what is right -not who is right?
<--- Score

10. Are there measurements based on task performance?
<--- Score

11. How can you measure the performance?
<--- Score

12. How do you stay flexible and focused to recognize

larger Microsoft Teams results?
<--- Score

13. What measurements are being captured?
<--- Score

14. How do you control the overall costs of your work processes?
<--- Score

15. What do you measure and why?
<--- Score

16. Financials: How Much Does it Really Cost?
<--- Score

17. Have all non-recommended alternatives been analyzed in sufficient detail?
<--- Score

18. What will the relative costs be?
<--- Score

19. How are measurements made?
<--- Score

20. The approach of traditional Microsoft Teams works for detail complexity but is focused on a systematic approach rather than an understanding of the nature of systems themselves, what approach will permit your organization to deal with the kind of unpredictable emergent behaviors that dynamic complexity can introduce?
<--- Score

21. Are high impact defects defined and identified in

the business process?
<--- Score

22. What is the right balance of time and resources between investigation, analysis, and discussion and dissemination?
<--- Score

23. How is progress measured?
<--- Score

24. Can you do Microsoft Teams without complex (expensive) analysis?
<--- Score

25. Have you made assumptions about the shape of the future, particularly its impact on your customers and competitors?
<--- Score

26. What methods are feasible and acceptable to estimate the impact of reforms?
<--- Score

27. How will effects be measured?
<--- Score

28. How large is the gap between current performance and the customer-specified (goal) performance?
<--- Score

29. Did you tackle the cause or the symptom?
<--- Score

30. What are your customers expectations and

measures?
<--- Score

31. What could cause delays in the schedule?
<--- Score

32. What is measured? Why?
<--- Score

33. How do you identify and analyze stakeholders and their interests?
<--- Score

34. Have the types of risks that may impact Microsoft Teams been identified and analyzed?
<--- Score

35. How do you aggregate measures across priorities?
<--- Score

36. What potential environmental factors impact the Microsoft Teams effort?
<--- Score

37. Is it possible to estimate the impact of unanticipated complexity such as wrong or failed assumptions, feedback, etc. on proposed reforms?
<--- Score

38. How will measures be used to manage and adapt?
<--- Score

39. Does Microsoft Teams analysis show the relationships among important Microsoft Teams factors?
<--- Score

40. What are the agreed upon definitions of the high impact areas, defect(s), unit(s), and opportunities that will figure into the process capability metrics?
<--- Score

41. What are the costs of reform?
<--- Score

42. Are process variation components displayed/ communicated using suitable charts, graphs, plots?
<--- Score

43. What disadvantage does this cause for the user?
<--- Score

44. Are there any easy-to-implement alternatives to Microsoft Teams? Sometimes other solutions are available that do not require the cost implications of a full-blown project?
<--- Score

45. What is an unallowable cost?
<--- Score

46. Are the measurements objective?
<--- Score

47. Does Microsoft Teams systematically track and analyze outcomes for accountability and quality improvement?
<--- Score

48. Are the units of measure consistent?
<--- Score

49. Do you aggressively reward and promote the people who have the biggest impact on creating excellent Microsoft Teams services/products?
<--- Score

50. Are losses documented, analyzed, and remedial processes developed to prevent future losses?
<--- Score

51. What is the cost required to operate and maintain the application by the organization?
<--- Score

52. What evidence is there and what is measured?
<--- Score

53. How do you measure lifecycle phases?
<--- Score

54. What causes innovation to fail or succeed in your organization?
<--- Score

55. Are missed Microsoft Teams opportunities costing your organization money?
<--- Score

56. What would be a real cause for concern?
<--- Score

57. How to cause the change?
<--- Score

58. What are the types and number of measures to use?
<--- Score

59. What are your key Microsoft Teams indicators that you will measure, analyze and track?
<--- Score

60. Have the concerns of stakeholders to help identify and define potential barriers been obtained and analyzed?
<--- Score

61. What has the team done to assure the stability and accuracy of the measurement process?
<--- Score

62. Is data collection planned and executed?
<--- Score

63. Are you aware of what could cause a problem?
<--- Score

64. How do you measure success?
<--- Score

65. How will success or failure be measured?
<--- Score

66. Which stakeholder characteristics are analyzed?
<--- Score

67. Can you measure the return on analysis?
<--- Score

68. How is performance measured?
<--- Score

69. How can you measure Microsoft Teams in a

systematic way?

<--- Score

70. Is Process Variation Displayed/Communicated?

<--- Score

71. What measurements are possible, practicable and meaningful?

<--- Score

72. How do you measure variability?

<--- Score

73. What data was collected (past, present, future/ ongoing)?

<--- Score

74. Is there a Performance Baseline?

<--- Score

75. How will you measure your Microsoft Teams effectiveness?

<--- Score

76. How frequently do you track Microsoft Teams measures?

<--- Score

77. Are key measures identified and agreed upon?

<--- Score

78. Have changes been properly/adequately analyzed for effect?

<--- Score

79. Is key measure data collection planned

and executed, process variation displayed and communicated and performance baselined?
<--- Score

80. Is long term and short term variability accounted for?
<--- Score

81. What could cause you to change course?
<--- Score

82. Where is it measured?
<--- Score

83. How do you measure efficient delivery of Microsoft Teams services?
<--- Score

84. Do you effectively measure and reward individual and team performance?
<--- Score

85. Is the solution cost-effective?
<--- Score

86. What are the uncertainties surrounding estimates of impact?
<--- Score

87. Was a data collection plan established?
<--- Score

88. How is the value delivered by Microsoft Teams being measured?
<--- Score

89. How do you know that any Microsoft Teams analysis is complete and comprehensive?
<--- Score

90. Is a solid data collection plan established that includes measurement systems analysis?
<--- Score

91. Among the Microsoft Teams product and service cost to be estimated, which is considered hardest to estimate?
<--- Score

92. How do you do risk analysis of rare, cascading, catastrophic events?
<--- Score

93. How will your organization measure success?
<--- Score

94. What are your key Microsoft Teams organizational performance measures, including key short and longer-term financial measures?
<--- Score

95. What are the key input variables? What are the key process variables? What are the key output variables?
<--- Score

96. How will you measure success?
<--- Score

97. What key measures identified indicate the performance of the business process?
<--- Score

98. Are you taking your company in the direction of better and revenue or cheaper and cost?
<--- Score

99. What causes extra work or rework?
<--- Score

100. What causes mismanagement?
<--- Score

101. High Performance Computing (HPC) in the Cloud- Are there Cost Savings?
<--- Score

102. What are the costs and price models (e.g., per hour on demand, per hour reserved, market bidding) for each type of resource?
<--- Score

103. What particular quality tools did the team find helpful in establishing measurements?
<--- Score

104. Does your organization systematically track and analyze outcomes related for accountability and quality improvement?
<--- Score

105. Who should receive measurement reports?
<--- Score

106. What causes investor action?
<--- Score

107. Why do you expend time and effort to implement measurement, for whom?

<--- Score

108. Who participated in the data collection for measurements?
<--- Score

109. What harm might be caused?
<--- Score

110. Do staff have the necessary skills to collect, analyze, and report data?
<--- Score

111. Why do the measurements/indicators matter?
<--- Score

Add up total points for this section:
_____ = Total points for this section

Divided by: _____ (number of statements answered) = _____
Average score for this section

Transfer your score to the Microsoft Teams Index at the beginning of the Self-Assessment.

CRITERION #4: ANALYZE:

INTENT: Analyze causes, assumptions and hypotheses.

In my belief, the answer to this question is clearly defined:

5 Strongly Agree

4 Agree

3 Neutral

2 Disagree

1 Strongly Disagree

1. Is the suppliers process defined and controlled?
<--- Score

2. Is the performance gap determined?
<--- Score

3. How was the detailed process map generated, verified, and validated?
<--- Score

4. What successful thing are you doing today that may be blinding you to new growth opportunities?
<--- Score

5. How is Microsoft Teams data gathered?
<--- Score

6. What will drive Microsoft Teams change?
<--- Score

7. Is the Microsoft Teams process severely broken such that a re-design is necessary?
<--- Score

8. What Microsoft Teams data do you gather or use now?
<--- Score

9. Are gaps between current performance and the goal performance identified?
<--- Score

10. What controls do you have in place to protect data?
<--- Score

11. How do your work systems and key work processes relate to and capitalize on your core competencies?
<--- Score

12. Think about the functions involved in your Microsoft Teams project, what processes flow from these functions?
<--- Score

13. Were any designed experiments used to generate additional insight into the data analysis?
<--- Score

14. What did the team gain from developing a sub-process map?
<--- Score

15. Will all documents be migrated to OneDrive?
<--- Score

16. Were Pareto charts (or similar) used to portray the 'heavy hitters' (or key sources of variation)?
<--- Score

17. How do mission and objectives affect the Microsoft Teams processes of your organization?
<--- Score

18. What other organizational variables, such as reward systems or communication systems, affect the performance of this Microsoft Teams process?
<--- Score

19. What were the financial benefits resulting from any 'ground fruit or low-hanging fruit' (quick fixes)?
<--- Score

20. What are your key performance measures or indicators and in-process measures for the control and improvement of your Microsoft Teams processes?
<--- Score

21. Is the gap/opportunity displayed and communicated in financial terms?
<--- Score

22. Do your leaders quickly bounce back from setbacks?
<--- Score

23. What quality tools were used to get through the analyze phase?
<--- Score

24. How do you use Microsoft Teams data and information to support organizational decision making and innovation?
<--- Score

25. Have any additional benefits been identified that will result from closing all or most of the gaps?
<--- Score

26. Were there any improvement opportunities identified from the process analysis?
<--- Score

27. What are your Microsoft Teams processes?
<--- Score

28. Can OneDrive do real-time online collaboration?
<--- Score

29. Identify an operational issue in your organization. for example, could a particular task be done more quickly or more efficiently by Microsoft Teams?
<--- Score

30. Are Microsoft Teams changes recognized early enough to be approved through the regular process?

<--- Score

31. How do you measure the operational performance of your key work systems and processes, including productivity, cycle time, and other appropriate measures of process effectiveness, efficiency, and innovation?
<--- Score

32. Think about some of the processes you undertake within your organization, which do you own?
<--- Score

33. Record-keeping requirements flow from the records needed as inputs, outputs, controls and for transformation of a Microsoft Teams process. Are the records needed as inputs to the Microsoft Teams process available?
<--- Score

34. What migration tools do you use to move local data to the cloud, if any?
<--- Score

35. Can you add value to the current Microsoft Teams decision-making process (largely qualitative) by incorporating uncertainty modeling (more quantitative)?
<--- Score

36. Was a detailed process map created to amplify critical steps of the 'as is' business process?
<--- Score

37. How often will data be collected for measures?
<--- Score

38. What is your organizations process which leads to recognition of value generation?
<--- Score

39. How does the organization define, manage, and improve its Microsoft Teams processes?
<--- Score

40. What process should you select for improvement?
<--- Score

41. How do you identify specific Microsoft Teams investment opportunities and emerging trends?
<--- Score

42. What does the data say about the performance of the business process?
<--- Score

43. What data is gathered?
<--- Score

44. What other jobs or tasks affect the performance of the steps in the Microsoft Teams process?
<--- Score

45. Have the problem and goal statements been updated to reflect the additional knowledge gained from the analyze phase?
<--- Score

46. Was a cause-and-effect diagram used to explore the different types of causes (or sources of variation)?
<--- Score

47. How can I automate processes so it is easier to maintain and manage my applications in the cloud?

<--- Score

48. What are your best practices for minimizing Microsoft Teams project risk, while demonstrating incremental value and quick wins throughout the Microsoft Teams project lifecycle?

<--- Score

49. How will access databases be handled, local and network?

<--- Score

50. Do your contracts/agreements contain data security obligations?

<--- Score

51. What tools were used to generate the list of possible causes?

<--- Score

52. Did any value-added analysis or 'lean thinking' take place to identify some of the gaps shown on the 'as is' process map?

<--- Score

53. Do several people in different organizational units assist with the Microsoft Teams process?

<--- Score

54. What methods do you use to gather Microsoft Teams data?

<--- Score

55. What is the cost of poor quality as supported by the team's analysis?

<--- Score

56. Is Data and process analysis, root cause analysis and quantifying the gap/opportunity in place?

<--- Score

57. Do your employees have the opportunity to do what they do best everyday?

<--- Score

58. Is the required Microsoft Teams data gathered?

<--- Score

59. A compounding model resolution with available relevant data can often provide insight towards a solution methodology; which Microsoft Teams models, tools and techniques are necessary?

<--- Score

60. Did any additional data need to be collected?

<--- Score

61. Where is the data coming from to measure compliance?

<--- Score

62. Do you, as a leader, bounce back quickly from setbacks?

<--- Score

63. What tools were used to narrow the list of possible causes?

<--- Score

64. What were the crucial 'moments of truth' on the process map?
<--- Score

65. What conclusions were drawn from the team's data collection and analysis? How did the team reach these conclusions?
<--- Score

66. An organizationally feasible system request is one that considers the mission, goals and objectives of the organization. Key questions are: is the Microsoft Teams solution request practical and will it solve a problem or take advantage of an opportunity to achieve company goals?
<--- Score

67. Where is Microsoft Teams data gathered?
<--- Score

68. What are the revised rough estimates of the financial savings/opportunity for Microsoft Teams improvements?
<--- Score

69. What are your current levels and trends in key measures or indicators of Microsoft Teams product and process performance that are important to and directly serve your customers? How do these results compare with the performance of your competitors and other organizations with similar offerings?
<--- Score

70. How do you promote understanding that opportunity for improvement is not criticism of the status quo, or the people who created the status quo?

<--- Score

71. How is the way you as the leader think and process information affecting your organizational culture?
<--- Score

72. What are your current levels and trends in key Microsoft Teams measures or indicators of product and process performance that are important to and directly serve your customers?
<--- Score

73. What are the best opportunities for value improvement?
<--- Score

74. How do you implement and manage your work processes to ensure that they meet design requirements?
<--- Score

Add up total points for this section:
_____ = Total points for this section

Divided by: _____ (number of statements answered) = _____
Average score for this section

Transfer your score to the Microsoft Teams Index at the beginning of the Self-Assessment.

CRITERION #5: IMPROVE:

INTENT: Develop a practical solution. Innovate, establish and test the solution and to measure the results.

In my belief, the answer to this question is clearly defined:

5 Strongly Agree

4 Agree

3 Neutral

2 Disagree

1 Strongly Disagree

1. What went well, what should change, what can improve?
<--- Score

2. Is the measure of success for Microsoft Teams understandable to a variety of people?
<--- Score

3. How do you define the solutions' scope?

<--- Score

4. How can skill-level changes improve Microsoft Teams?
<--- Score

5. What communications are necessary to support the implementation of the solution?
<--- Score

6. Risk factors: what are the characteristics of Microsoft Teams that make it risky?
<--- Score

7. How will you know that you have improved?
<--- Score

8. Who will be responsible for making the decisions to include or exclude requested changes once Microsoft Teams is underway?
<--- Score

9. Is pilot data collected and analyzed?
<--- Score

10. Explorations of the frontiers of Microsoft Teams will help you build influence, improve Microsoft Teams, optimize decision making, and sustain change, what is your approach?
<--- Score

11. Are possible solutions generated and tested?
<--- Score

12. What were the underlying assumptions on the cost-benefit analysis?

<--- Score

13. How do you keep improving Microsoft Teams?
<--- Score

14. How does the team improve its work?
<--- Score

15. Is supporting Microsoft Teams documentation required?
<--- Score

16. How significant is the improvement in the eyes of the end user?
<--- Score

17. What tools were used to tap into the creativity and encourage 'outside the box' thinking?
<--- Score

18. What needs improvement? Why?
<--- Score

19. Is a contingency plan established?
<--- Score

20. Are risk triggers captured?
<--- Score

21. How did the team generate the list of possible solutions?
<--- Score

22. What attendant changes will need to be made to ensure that the solution is successful?
<--- Score

23. What lessons, if any, from a pilot were incorporated into the design of the full-scale solution?
<--- Score

24. Were any criteria developed to assist the team in testing and evaluating potential solutions?
<--- Score

25. Are the best solutions selected?
<--- Score

26. How can you improve Microsoft Teams?
<--- Score

27. What is my overall risk tolerance?
<--- Score

28. What actually has to improve and by how much?
<--- Score

29. How will you measure the results?
<--- Score

30. Can the solution be designed and implemented within an acceptable time period?
<--- Score

31. Desired Outcomes: What do we want to accomplish as the end result of this contract?
<--- Score

32. Is there a high likelihood that any recommendations will achieve their intended results?
<--- Score

33. Why improve in the first place?
<--- Score

34. Are improved process ('should be') maps modified based on pilot data and analysis?
<--- Score

35. How do you go about comparing Microsoft Teams approaches/solutions?
<--- Score

36. Is a solution implementation plan established, including schedule/work breakdown structure, resources, risk management plan, cost/budget, and control plan?
<--- Score

37. How do you measure improved Microsoft Teams service perception, and satisfaction?
<--- Score

38. What is the implementation plan?
<--- Score

39. How can I improve the efficiency (and reduce waste) in my deployment footprint?
<--- Score

40. What to do with the results or outcomes of measurements?
<--- Score

41. Is the implementation plan designed?
<--- Score

42. Will the controls trigger any other risks?

<--- Score

43. What is the Microsoft Teams's sustainability risk?
<--- Score

44. To what extent does management recognize Microsoft Teams as a tool to increase the results?
<--- Score

45. Who will be responsible for documenting the Microsoft Teams requirements in detail?
<--- Score

46. Which of the recognised risks out of all risks can be most likely transferred?
<--- Score

47. How can you improve performance?
<--- Score

48. Who controls the risk?
<--- Score

49. How do you measure risk?
<--- Score

50. How will the team or the process owner(s) monitor the implementation plan to see that it is working as intended?
<--- Score

51. Are new and improved process ('should be') maps developed?
<--- Score

52. Are there any constraints (technical, political,

cultural, or otherwise) that would inhibit certain solutions?
<--- Score

53. Is the solution technically practical?
<--- Score

54. Was a pilot designed for the proposed solution(s)?
<--- Score

55. Do those selected for the Microsoft Teams team have a good general understanding of what Microsoft Teams is all about?
<--- Score

56. What are your current levels and trends in key measures or indicators of workforce and leader development?
<--- Score

57. What is the team's contingency plan for potential problems occurring in implementation?
<--- Score

58. Who will be using the results of the measurement activities?
<--- Score

59. Can you identify any significant risks or exposures to Microsoft Teams third- parties (vendors, service providers, alliance partners etc) that concern you?
<--- Score

60. What are the potential risks?
<--- Score

61. What do you want to improve?
<--- Score

62. How do you manage and improve your Microsoft Teams work systems to deliver customer value and achieve organizational success and sustainability?
<--- Score

63. If you could go back in time five years, what decision would you make differently? What is your best guess as to what decision you're making today you might regret five years from now?
<--- Score

64. How do you link measurement and risk?
<--- Score

65. How does the solution remove the key sources of issues discovered in the analyze phase?
<--- Score

66. Describe the design of the pilot and what tests were conducted, if any?
<--- Score

67. What improvements have been achieved?
<--- Score

68. What should a proof of concept or pilot accomplish?
<--- Score

69. How do the Microsoft Teams results compare with the performance of your competitors and other organizations with similar offerings?
<--- Score

70. What does the 'should be' process map/design look like?
<--- Score

71. Who controls key decisions that will be made?
<--- Score

72. What tools were most useful during the improve phase?
<--- Score

73. What tools were used to evaluate the potential solutions?
<--- Score

74. For decision problems, how do you develop a decision statement?
<--- Score

75. What can you do to improve?
<--- Score

76. Are you assessing Microsoft Teams and risk?
<--- Score

77. Risk events: what are the things that could go wrong?
<--- Score

78. How will you know when its improved?
<--- Score

79. What is the magnitude of the improvements?
<--- Score

80. How will the organization know that the solution worked?
<--- Score

81. What resources are required for the improvement efforts?
<--- Score

82. Is the scope clearly documented?
<--- Score

83. How do you measure progress and evaluate training effectiveness?
<--- Score

84. What practices helps your organization to develop its capacity to recognize patterns?
<--- Score

85. What error proofing will be done to address some of the discrepancies observed in the 'as is' process?
<--- Score

86. Is there a cost/benefit analysis of optimal solution(s)?
<--- Score

87. In the past few months, what is the smallest change you have made that has had the biggest positive result? What was it about that small change that produced the large return?
<--- Score

88. Is there a small-scale pilot for proposed improvement(s)? What conclusions were drawn from the outcomes of a pilot?

<--- Score

89. For estimation problems, how do you develop an estimation statement?
<--- Score

90. Who are the people involved in developing and implementing Microsoft Teams?
<--- Score

91. How do you improve productivity?
<--- Score

92. What is the risk?
<--- Score

93. What is Microsoft Teams's impact on utilizing the best solution(s)?
<--- Score

94. What are the implications of the one critical Microsoft Teams decision 10 minutes, 10 months, and 10 years from now?
<--- Score

95. How do you improve your likelihood of success ?
<--- Score

96. Does the goal represent a desired result that can be measured?
<--- Score

97. Required Service: What task must be accomplished to give us the desired result?
<--- Score

98. Is the optimal solution selected based on testing and analysis?
<--- Score

99. Risk Identification: What are the possible risk events your organization faces in relation to Microsoft Teams?
<--- Score

100. How do you improve Microsoft Teams service perception, and satisfaction?
<--- Score

101. How will you know that a change is an improvement?
<--- Score

Add up total points for this section:
_____ = Total points for this section

Divided by: _____ (number of
statements answered) = _____
Average score for this section

Transfer your score to the Microsoft
Teams Index at the beginning of the
Self-Assessment.

CRITERION #6: CONTROL:

INTENT: Implement the practical solution. Maintain the performance and correct possible complications.

In my belief, the answer to this question is clearly defined:

5 Strongly Agree

4 Agree

3 Neutral

2 Disagree

1 Strongly Disagree

1. Have new or revised work instructions resulted?
<--- Score

2. Has the improved process and its steps been standardized?
<--- Score

3. How do you plan on providing proper recognition and disclosure of supporting companies?

<--- Score

4. How likely is the current Microsoft Teams plan to come in on schedule or on budget?
<--- Score

5. Where do ideas that reach policy makers and planners as proposals for Microsoft Teams strengthening and reform actually originate?
<--- Score

6. What adjustments to the strategies are needed?
<--- Score

7. How will report readings be checked to effectively monitor performance?
<--- Score

8. Do you monitor the effectiveness of your Microsoft Teams activities?
<--- Score

9. How might the organization capture best practices and lessons learned so as to leverage improvements across the business?
<--- Score

10. Act/Adjust: What Do you Need to Do Differently?
<--- Score

11. Is there a control plan in place for sustaining improvements (short and long-term)?
<--- Score

12. Are the planned controls in place?
<--- Score

13. What key inputs and outputs are being measured on an ongoing basis?
<--- Score

14. Who is the Microsoft Teams process owner?
<--- Score

15. What is the best design framework for Microsoft Teams organization now that, in a post industrial-age if the top-down, command and control model is no longer relevant?
<--- Score

16. Are operating procedures consistent?
<--- Score

17. Are pertinent alerts monitored, analyzed and distributed to appropriate personnel?
<--- Score

18. How do senior leaders actions reflect a commitment to the organizations Microsoft Teams values?
<--- Score

19. Is there a Microsoft Teams Communication plan covering who needs to get what information when?
<--- Score

20. Is there a standardized process?
<--- Score

21. Implementation Planning: is a pilot needed to test the changes before a full roll out occurs?
<--- Score

22. Will the team be available to assist members in planning investigations?
<--- Score

23. In the case of a Microsoft Teams project, the criteria for the audit derive from implementation objectives. an audit of a Microsoft Teams project involves assessing whether the recommendations outlined for implementation have been met. Can you track that any Microsoft Teams project is implemented as planned, and is it working?
<--- Score

24. Do the Microsoft Teams decisions you make today help people and the planet tomorrow?
<--- Score

25. How do you establish and deploy modified action plans if circumstances require a shift in plans and rapid execution of new plans?
<--- Score

26. Who controls critical resources?
<--- Score

27. Are the planned controls working?
<--- Score

28. How do controls support value?
<--- Score

29. Who will be in control?
<--- Score

30. How do you select, collect, align, and integrate

Microsoft Teams data and information for tracking daily operations and overall organizational performance, including progress relative to strategic objectives and action plans?

<--- Score

31. How will the process owner verify improvement in present and future sigma levels, process capabilities?

<--- Score

32. Is there a documented and implemented monitoring plan?

<--- Score

33. Is there a recommended audit plan for routine surveillance inspections of Microsoft Teams's gains?

<--- Score

34. What is your theory of human motivation, and how does your compensation plan fit with that view?

<--- Score

35. What is the opportunity cost of providing staff with the potential to learn new technologies or increase their expertise?

<--- Score

36. Do you monitor the Microsoft Teams decisions made and fine tune them as they evolve?

<--- Score

37. What are the known security controls?

<--- Score

38. What can you control?

<--- Score

39. How is change control managed?
<--- Score

40. What should you measure to verify efficiency gains?
<--- Score

41. How can you best use all of your knowledge repositories to enhance learning and sharing?
<--- Score

42. You may have created your quality measures at a time when you lacked resources, technology wasn't up to the required standard, or low service levels were the industry norm. Have those circumstances changed?
<--- Score

43. How will you measure your QA plan's effectiveness?
<--- Score

44. Who is doing any particular monitoring or auditing task?
<--- Score

45. Can support from partners be adjusted?
<--- Score

46. Does the Microsoft Teams performance meet the customer's requirements?
<--- Score

47. What are the key elements of your Microsoft Teams performance improvement system, including

your evaluation, organizational learning, and innovation processes?
<--- Score

48. Is reporting being used or needed?
<--- Score

49. Who has control over resources?
<--- Score

50. What should the next improvement project be that is related to Microsoft Teams?
<--- Score

51. How will input, process, and output variables be checked to detect for sub-optimal conditions?
<--- Score

52. Are suggested corrective/restorative actions indicated on the response plan for known causes to problems that might surface?
<--- Score

53. Who sets the Microsoft Teams standards?
<--- Score

54. How will new or emerging customer needs/requirements be checked/communicated to orient the process toward meeting the new specifications and continually reducing variation?
<--- Score

55. Are new process steps, standards, and documentation ingrained into normal operations?
<--- Score

56. Is a response plan established and deployed?
<--- Score

57. Will your goals reflect your program budget?
<--- Score

58. Are controls in place and consistently applied?
<--- Score

59. Is knowledge gained on process shared and institutionalized?
<--- Score

60. Does the response plan contain a definite closed loop continual improvement scheme (e.g., plan-do-check-act)?
<--- Score

61. What quality tools were useful in the control phase?
<--- Score

62. Are there documented procedures?
<--- Score

63. What do you measure to verify effectiveness gains?
<--- Score

64. Monitoring Method: How will we determine that success has been achieved?
<--- Score

65. Are you measuring, monitoring and predicting Microsoft Teams activities to optimize operations and profitability, and enhancing outcomes?

<--- Score

66. Did I learn the basic AWS terminology (instances, AMIs, volumes, snapshots, distributions, domains and so on)?
<--- Score

67. Is a response plan in place for when the input, process, or output measures indicate an 'out-of-control' condition?
<--- Score

68. Are documented procedures clear and easy to follow for the operators?
<--- Score

69. How will the day-to-day responsibilities for monitoring and continual improvement be transferred from the improvement team to the process owner?
<--- Score

70. Against what alternative is success being measured?
<--- Score

71. How do your controls stack up?
<--- Score

72. What is the control/monitoring plan?
<--- Score

73. Who is informed of the results of a particular monitoring or auditing task, and when?
<--- Score

74. Is there a transfer of ownership and knowledge to process owner and process team tasked with the responsibilities.
<--- Score

75. How will the process owner and team be able to hold the gains?
<--- Score

76. What do your reports reflect?
<--- Score

77. Can you adapt and adjust to changing Microsoft Teams situations?
<--- Score

78. What other areas of the organization might benefit from the Microsoft Teams team's improvements, knowledge, and learning?
<--- Score

79. Is there documentation that will support the successful operation of the improvement?
<--- Score

80. What are the critical parameters to watch?
<--- Score

81. Is new knowledge gained imbedded in the response plan?
<--- Score

82. Will any special training be provided for results interpretation?
<--- Score

83. Does a troubleshooting guide exist or is it needed?
<--- Score

84. What are you attempting to measure/monitor?
<--- Score

85. What do you stand for--and what are you against?
<--- Score

86. What is the recommended frequency of auditing?
<--- Score

87. Does Microsoft Teams appropriately measure and monitor risk?
<--- Score

88. How do you encourage people to take control and responsibility?
<--- Score

89. Does job training on the documented procedures need to be part of the process team's education and training?
<--- Score

90. What other systems, operations, processes, and infrastructures (hiring practices, staffing, training, incentives/rewards, metrics/dashboards/scorecards, etc.) need updates, additions, changes, or deletions in order to facilitate knowledge transfer and improvements?
<--- Score

Add up total points for this section:
_____ = Total points for this section

Divided by: _____ (number of
statements answered) = _____
Average score for this section

Transfer your score to the Microsoft
Teams Index at the beginning of the
Self-Assessment.

CRITERION #7: SUSTAIN:

INTENT: Retain the benefits.

In my belief, the answer to this question is clearly defined:

5 Strongly Agree

4 Agree

3 Neutral

2 Disagree

1 Strongly Disagree

1. Which functions and people interact with the supplier and or customer?
<--- Score

2. What is your responsibility?
<--- Score

3. What is your question? Why?
<--- Score

4. Which individuals, teams or departments will be

involved in Microsoft Teams?

<--- Score

5. What is the purpose of Microsoft Teams in relation to the mission?

<--- Score

6. What are you challenging?

<--- Score

7. Why should you adopt a Microsoft Teams framework?

<--- Score

8. What would have to be true for the option on the table to be the best possible choice?

<--- Score

9. What would you recommend your friend do if he/she were facing this dilemma?

<--- Score

10. Who do we want your customers to become?

<--- Score

11. Do you have the right capabilities and capacities?

<--- Score

12. Who, on the executive team or the board, has spoken to a customer recently?

<--- Score

13. Are you making progress, and are you making progress as Microsoft Teams leaders?

<--- Score

14. What have you done to protect your business from competitive encroachment?
<--- Score

15. Is the Microsoft Teams organization completing tasks effectively and efficiently?
<--- Score

16. Can you maintain your growth without detracting from the factors that have contributed to your success?
<--- Score

17. What information should be included?
<--- Score

18. How do you create buy-in?
<--- Score

19. What is your BATNA (best alternative to a negotiated agreement)?
<--- Score

20. What should you stop doing?
<--- Score

21. What are the dependencies between the application being migrated and other systems?
<--- Score

22. Why is it important to have senior management support for a Microsoft Teams project?
<--- Score

23. Are room reservations/scheduling available in Office 365?

<--- Score

24. How can I take advantage of some of the other advanced AWS features and services?

<--- Score

25. Are the licensing/subscriptions tied to machines or individuals?

<--- Score

26. What business benefits will Microsoft Teams goals deliver if achieved?

<--- Score

27. What are the pricing options and considerations?

<--- Score

28. Which business applications should move to the cloud first?

<--- Score

29. Who are four people whose careers you have enhanced?

<--- Score

30. How much contingency will be available in the budget?

<--- Score

31. What are the rules and assumptions your industry operates under? What if the opposite were true?

<--- Score

32. Was there training?

<--- Score

33. Can the schedule be done in the given time?
<--- Score

34. What trophy do you want on your mantle?
<--- Score

35. Who have you, as a company, historically been when you've been at your best?
<--- Score

36. How do you lead with Microsoft Teams in mind?
<--- Score

37. Ask yourself: how would you do this work if you only had one staff member to do it?
<--- Score

38. Were lessons learned captured and communicated?
<--- Score

39. What are the different type of migration and main migration tasks involved?
<--- Score

40. What are the potential basics of Microsoft Teams fraud?
<--- Score

41. How do you foster innovation?
<--- Score

42. What role does communication play in the success or failure of a Microsoft Teams project?
<--- Score

43. How can you negotiate Microsoft Teams successfully with a stubborn boss, an irate client, or a deceitful coworker?

<--- Score

44. What web browsers are supported?

<--- Score

45. Will there be any necessary staff changes (redundancies or new hires)?

<--- Score

46. Are the assumptions believable and achievable?

<--- Score

47. How can you protect yourself from malware that could be introduced by another customer in a multi-tenant environment?

<--- Score

48. Do you have enough freaky customers in your portfolio pushing you to the limit day in and day out?

<--- Score

49. How do you manage Microsoft Teams Knowledge Management (KM)?

<--- Score

50. How is implementation research currently incorporated into each of your goals?

<--- Score

51. What are the success criteria that will indicate that Microsoft Teams objectives have been met and the benefits delivered?

<--- Score

52. Who do you want your customers to become?
<--- Score

53. Is custom code allowed in SharePoint online?
<--- Score

54. What knowledge, skills and characteristics mark a good Microsoft Teams project manager?
<--- Score

55. Are you maintaining a past–present–future perspective throughout the Microsoft Teams discussion?
<--- Score

56. Why do and why don't your customers like your organization?
<--- Score

57. What is the source of the strategies for Microsoft Teams strengthening and reform?
<--- Score

58. How can you become the company that would put you out of business?
<--- Score

59. What kind of crime could a potential new hire have committed that would not only not disqualify him/her from being hired by your organization, but would actually indicate that he/she might be a particularly good fit?
<--- Score

60. What special considerations have you made?
<--- Score

61. How will you ensure you get what you expected?
<--- Score

62. What are the short and long-term Microsoft Teams goals?
<--- Score

63. If you were responsible for initiating and implementing major changes in your organization, what steps might you take to ensure acceptance of those changes?
<--- Score

64. How do you go about securing Microsoft Teams?
<--- Score

65. What are the barriers to increased Microsoft Teams production?
<--- Score

66. How do you foster the skills, knowledge, talents, attributes, and characteristics you want to have?
<--- Score

67. What is an unauthorized commitment?
<--- Score

68. Who is the main stakeholder, with ultimate responsibility for driving Microsoft Teams forward?
<--- Score

69. What information is critical to your organization that your executives are ignoring?

<--- Score

70. How do you listen to customers to obtain actionable information?
<--- Score

71. Where should your aim be?
<--- Score

72. What is the range of capabilities?
<--- Score

73. How does Microsoft Teams integrate with other business initiatives?
<--- Score

74. Are you paying enough attention to the partners your company depends on to succeed?
<--- Score

75. Are new benefits received and understood?
<--- Score

76. What is the recommended frequency of auditing?
<--- Score

77. Do you have an implicit bias for capital investments over people investments?
<--- Score

78. Do you see more potential in people than they do in themselves?
<--- Score

79. Which cloud types to select?
<--- Score

80. To whom do you add value?
<--- Score

81. Is Microsoft Teams realistic, or are you setting yourself up for failure?
<--- Score

82. What are the top 3 things at the forefront of your Microsoft Teams agendas for the next 3 years?
<--- Score

83. More expensive in the long run?
<--- Score

84. Who will manage the integration of tools?
<--- Score

85. In a project to restructure Microsoft Teams outcomes, which stakeholders would you involve?
<--- Score

86. How do you keep records, of what?
<--- Score

87. Are there third party components or other supporting components that are not compatible with the selected platform?
<--- Score

88. What does your signature ensure?
<--- Score

89. Who will determine interim and final deadlines?
<--- Score

90. How can we get rid of support contracts for hardware, software and network?

<--- Score

91. What Microsoft Teams modifications can you make work for you?

<--- Score

92. What are the challenges?

<--- Score

93. Have new benefits been realized?

<--- Score

94. Do you think Microsoft Teams accomplishes the goals you expect it to accomplish?

<--- Score

95. Now that I have migrated existing applications, what else can I do in order to leverage the elasticity and scalability benefits that the cloud promises?

<--- Score

96. Did your employees make progress today?

<--- Score

97. Which license should you buy?

<--- Score

98. What new services of functionality will be implemented next with Microsoft Teams ?

<--- Score

99. Is the Cloud FERPA, HIPAA, and FISMA compliant?

<--- Score

100. Is there any reason to believe the opposite of my current belief?
<--- Score

101. What are internal and external Microsoft Teams relations?
<--- Score

102. How will you know that the Microsoft Teams project has been successful?
<--- Score

103. What stupid rule would you most like to kill?
<--- Score

104. Would you rather sell to knowledgeable and informed customers or to uninformed customers?
<--- Score

105. Which models, tools and techniques are necessary?
<--- Score

106. Are there any disadvantages to implementing Microsoft Teams? There might be some that are less obvious?
<--- Score

107. What is it like to work for you?
<--- Score

108. What did you miss in the interview for the worst hire you ever made?
<--- Score

109. How does the organization acquire and allocate its computing resources?
<--- Score

110. What are current Microsoft Teams paradigms?
<--- Score

111. What must you excel at?
<--- Score

112. If you had to leave your organization for a year and the only communication you could have with employees/colleagues was a single paragraph, what would you write?
<--- Score

113. Who is on the team?
<--- Score

114. Acceptable Quality Level (AQL): How much error will we accept?
<--- Score

115. How important is Microsoft Teams to the user organizations mission?
<--- Score

116. Are assumptions made in Microsoft Teams stated explicitly?
<--- Score

117. What unique value proposition (UVP) do you offer?
<--- Score

118. Can you break it down?
<--- Score

119. How long will it take to change?
<--- Score

120. Are you be able to share/delegate calendar viewing in Office 365?
<--- Score

121. What Microsoft Teams skills are most important?
<--- Score

122. Is it economical; do you have the time and money?
<--- Score

123. Are you satisfied with your current role? If not, what is missing from it?
<--- Score

124. Will the organization business benefit from the migration?
<--- Score

125. Is mobile device management included in Office 365?
<--- Score

126. Marketing budgets are tighter, consumers are more skeptical, and social media has changed forever the way we talk about Microsoft Teams. How do you gain traction?
<--- Score

127. What potential megatrends could make your

business model obsolete?
<--- Score

128. When information truly is ubiquitous, when reach and connectivity are completely global, when computing resources are infinite, and when a whole new set of impossibilities are not only possible, but happening, what will that do to your business?
<--- Score

129. How much does Microsoft Teams help?
<--- Score

130. Think of your Microsoft Teams project, what are the main functions?
<--- Score

131. Who do you think the world wants your organization to be?
<--- Score

132. How do you govern and fulfill your societal responsibilities?
<--- Score

133. Whom among your colleagues do you trust, and for what?
<--- Score

134. If you weren't already in this business, would you enter it today? And if not, what are you going to do about it?
<--- Score

135. Can you package and deploy your application into an AMI so it can run on an Amazon EC2

instance?
<--- Score

136. What strategies are most appropriate for the migration effort?
<--- Score

137. What are the usability implications of Microsoft Teams actions?
<--- Score

138. Whose voice (department, ethnic group, women, older workers, etc) might you have missed hearing from in your company, and how might you amplify this voice to create positive momentum for your business?
<--- Score

139. What relationships among Microsoft Teams trends do you perceive?
<--- Score

140. Who are the key stakeholders?
<--- Score

141. When you map the key players in your own work and the types/domains of relationships with them, which relationships do you find easy and which challenging, and why?
<--- Score

142. Do the licensing/subscriptions allow for installation on multiple devices per user?
<--- Score

143. In retrospect, of the projects that you pulled the

plug on, what percent do you wish had been allowed to keep going, and what percent do you wish had ended earlier?
<--- Score

144. Will this affect mailbox delegations?
<--- Score

145. Which Microsoft Teams goals are the most important?
<--- Score

146. How likely is it that a customer would recommend your company to a friend or colleague?
<--- Score

147. Do you feel that more should be done in the Microsoft Teams area?
<--- Score

148. How can your organization effectively and efficiently absorb new technology?
<--- Score

149. Do you have past Microsoft Teams successes?
<--- Score

150. What projects are going on in the organization today, and what resources are those projects using from the resource pools?
<--- Score

151. Do you say no to customers for no reason?
<--- Score

152. What are some challenges involved in

migrating to the cloud?

<--- Score

153. How do you assess the Microsoft Teams pitfalls that are inherent in implementing it?

<--- Score

154. Who is responsible for errors?

<--- Score

155. Who else should you help?

<--- Score

156. Are all key stakeholders present at all Structured Walkthroughs?

<--- Score

157. Is it possible to isolate the components using Amazon SQS?

<--- Score

158. High Performance Computing (HPC) in the Cloud- What are the Gaps?

<--- Score

159. Can you extract stateful components and make them stateless?

<--- Score

160. What may be the consequences for the performance of an organization if all stakeholders are not consulted regarding Microsoft Teams?

<--- Score

161. Have benefits been optimized with all key stakeholders?

<--- Score

162. How do you keep the momentum going?
<--- Score

163. Does Office 365 or Outlook block certain file types?
<--- Score

164. How do you engage the workforce, in addition to satisfying them?
<--- Score

165. What was the last experiment you ran?
<--- Score

166. Are the criteria for selecting recommendations stated?
<--- Score

167. What are the existing tasks, methods and techniques to enable migration of legacy on-premise software to the cloud?
<--- Score

168. Are you using a design thinking approach and integrating Innovation, Microsoft Teams Experience, and Brand Value?
<--- Score

169. What is the funding source for this project?
<--- Score

170. How do you make it meaningful in connecting Microsoft Teams with what users do day-to-day?
<--- Score

171. Political -is anyone trying to undermine this project?
<--- Score

172. What are the business goals Microsoft Teams is aiming to achieve?
<--- Score

173. Can you do all this work?
<--- Score

174. How do customers see your organization?
<--- Score

175. How do you set Microsoft Teams stretch targets and how do you get people to not only participate in setting these stretch targets but also that they strive to achieve these?
<--- Score

176. Do you have the right people on the bus?
<--- Score

177. Will it be accepted by users?
<--- Score

178. Why is Microsoft Teams important for you now?
<--- Score

179. Who is responsible for ensuring appropriate resources (time, people and money) are allocated to Microsoft Teams?
<--- Score

180. How do you cross-sell and up-sell your Microsoft

Teams success?

<--- Score

181. Are you changing as fast as the world around you?

<--- Score

182. What do we do when new problems arise?

<--- Score

183. Have You Got the Right Tools?

<--- Score

184. How do you deal with Microsoft Teams changes?

<--- Score

185. What happens when a new employee joins the organization?

<--- Score

186. What is the kind of project structure that would be appropriate for your Microsoft Teams project, should it be formal and complex, or can it be less formal and relatively simple?

<--- Score

187. What one word do you want to own in the minds of your customers, employees, and partners?

<--- Score

188. What sorts of activities must be performed to accomplish the migration?

<--- Score

189. If your company went out of business tomorrow, would anyone who doesn't get a paycheck here care?

<--- Score

190. What are the long-term Microsoft Teams goals?
<--- Score

191. Is the impact that Microsoft Teams has shown?
<--- Score

192. What additional Office 365 modules are available that you may want?
<--- Score

193. Is the application owner willing and comfortable with a cloud platform?
<--- Score

194. Who are your customers?
<--- Score

195. Why not do Microsoft Teams?
<--- Score

196. How will you insure seamless interoperability of Microsoft Teams moving forward?
<--- Score

197. Single point of failure / compromise?
<--- Score

198. What are the key enablers to make this Microsoft Teams move?
<--- Score

199. What are you trying to prove to yourself, and how might it be hijacking your life and business success?
<--- Score

200. Do you think you know, or do you know you know ?
<--- Score

201. Do Microsoft Teams rules make a reasonable demand on a users capabilities?
<--- Score

202. What are the gaps in your knowledge and experience?
<--- Score

203. What is getting in your way of doing work?
<--- Score

204. What are specific Microsoft Teams rules to follow?
<--- Score

205. How can you become more high-tech but still be high touch?
<--- Score

206. Who will provide the final approval of Microsoft Teams deliverables?
<--- Score

207. Who will be responsible for deciding whether Microsoft Teams goes ahead or not after the initial investigations?
<--- Score

208. What are your most important goals for the strategic Microsoft Teams objectives?
<--- Score

209. What have you done since the last Daily Scrum?

<--- Score

210. How are you doing compared to your industry?

<--- Score

211. What you are going to do to affect the numbers?

<--- Score

212. What is the craziest thing you can do?

<--- Score

213. Are you / should you be revolutionary or evolutionary?

<--- Score

214. Where can you break convention?

<--- Score

215. Instead of going to current contacts for new ideas, what if you reconnected with dormant contacts--the people you used to know? If you were going reactivate a dormant tie, who would it be?

<--- Score

216. What are the main practical motivations behind legacy migrations to the cloud?

<--- Score

217. Why should people listen to you?

<--- Score

218. Is a Microsoft Teams team work effort in place?

<--- Score

219. What is the estimated value of the project?
<--- Score

220. How will you motivate the stakeholders with the least vested interest?
<--- Score

221. Why will customers want to buy your organizations products/services?
<--- Score

222. Can you divide the application into components and run them on separate Amazon EC2 instances?
<--- Score

223. How do you authorize an employee to access a system or application in the cloud?
<--- Score

224. What are your personal philosophies regarding Microsoft Teams and how do they influence your work?
<--- Score

225. Operational - will it work?
<--- Score

226. How can I move part of or an entire system to the cloud without disrupting or interrupting my current business?
<--- Score

227. What will be the consequences to the stakeholder (financial, reputation etc) if Microsoft Teams does not go ahead or fails to deliver the

objectives?
<--- Score

228. Who is my regularly servicing acquisition office?
<--- Score

229. Should I be using the cloud or not?
<--- Score

230. Is the migration staff experienced with the technologies available on the cloud platform?
<--- Score

231. Are your responses positive or negative?
<--- Score

232. How do phones that work with Skype for Business today work with Microsoft Teams?
<--- Score

233. Are limitations and future implications for cloud migration clearly positioned?
<--- Score

234. If you got fired and a new hire took your place, what would she do different?
<--- Score

235. How do you decide how much to remunerate an employee?
<--- Score

236. What threat is Microsoft Teams addressing?
<--- Score

237. How do you ensure that implementations of Microsoft Teams products are done in a way that ensures safety?
<--- Score

238. Has implementation been effective in reaching specified objectives so far?
<--- Score

239. If there were zero limitations, what would you do differently?
<--- Score

240. Are there any activities that you can take off your to do list?
<--- Score

241. Is there a work around that you can use?
<--- Score

242. What happens if you do not have enough funding?
<--- Score

243. In the past year, what have you done (or could you have done) to increase the accurate perception of your company/brand as ethical and honest?
<--- Score

244. How do you track customer value, profitability or financial return, organizational success, and sustainability?
<--- Score

245. If your customer were your grandmother, would you tell her to buy what you're selling?

<--- Score

246. What are the existing methods, techniques and tool support to enable migration of legacy software towards cloud-based environment?
<--- Score

247. What is your formula for success in Microsoft Teams ?
<--- Score

248. Which component must be local (on-premise) and which can move to the cloud?
<--- Score

249. What is a feasible sequencing of reform initiatives over time?
<--- Score

250. How can I instrument my applications to have more visibility of my deployed applications?
<--- Score

251. What happens at your organization when people fail?
<--- Score

252. What have been your experiences in defining long range Microsoft Teams goals?
<--- Score

253. What is the motivation that led the organization to contemplate cloud migration?
<--- Score

254. How are companies leveraging the cloud

across the organization?
<--- Score

255. What are strategies for increasing support and reducing opposition?
<--- Score

256. Who uses your product in ways you never expected?
<--- Score

257. How do you maintain Microsoft Teams's Integrity?
<--- Score

258. What counts that you are not counting?
<--- Score

259. At what moment would you think; Will I get fired?
<--- Score

260. What current systems have to be understood and/or changed?
<--- Score

261. Is maximizing Microsoft Teams protection the same as minimizing Microsoft Teams loss?
<--- Score

262. What are the essentials of internal Microsoft Teams management?
<--- Score

263. How do you stay inspired?
<--- Score

264. What are the main practical motivations

behind legacy migrations towards the cloud?
<--- Score

265. What management system can you use to leverage the Microsoft Teams experience, ideas, and concerns of the people closest to the work to be done?
<--- Score

266. What is effective Microsoft Teams?
<--- Score

267. Are there regional teams established and who manages and requests the assets?
<--- Score

268. What is the experience level of the organizations IT professionals, including their ability to negotiate and engage in technical discussions in a foreign language (particularly for non English speakers)?
<--- Score

269. How do you determine the key elements that affect Microsoft Teams workforce satisfaction, how are these elements determined for different workforce groups and segments?
<--- Score

270. What is your competitive advantage?
<--- Score

271. What goals did you miss?
<--- Score

272. How can you incorporate support to ensure safe

and effective use of Microsoft Teams into the services that you provide?
<--- Score

273. What trouble can you get into?
<--- Score

274. How do you transition from the baseline to the target?
<--- Score

275. How do you know if you are successful?
<--- Score

276. Are you relevant? Will you be relevant five years from now? Ten?
<--- Score

277. How do you proactively clarify deliverables and Microsoft Teams quality expectations?
<--- Score

278. What is something you believe that nearly no one agrees with you on?
<--- Score

279. Do you know what you are doing? And who do you call if you don't?
<--- Score

280. How do you accomplish your long range Microsoft Teams goals?
<--- Score

281. How do you provide a safe environment -physically and emotionally?

<--- Score

282. Who is responsible for Microsoft Teams?
<--- Score

283. If you do not follow, then how to lead?
<--- Score

284. If no one would ever find out about your accomplishments, how would you lead differently?
<--- Score

285. Is your basic point _____ or _____?
<--- Score

286. Is Microsoft Teams dependent on the successful delivery of a current project?
<--- Score

Add up total points for this section:
_____ = Total points for this section

Divided by: _____ (number of statements answered) = _____
Average score for this section

Transfer your score to the Microsoft Teams Index at the beginning of the Self-Assessment.

Microsoft Teams and Managing Projects, Criteria for Project Managers:

1.0 Initiating Process Group: Microsoft Teams

1. Were escalated issues resolved promptly?

2. When will the Microsoft Teams project be done?

3. Who is funding the Microsoft Teams project?

4. Have the stakeholders identified all individual requirements pertaining to business process?

5. What do you need to do?

6. Specific - is the objective clear in terms of what, how, when, and where the situation will be changed?

7. How will you know you did it?

8. What were things that you did well, and could improve, and how?

9. Information sharing?

10. Where must it be done?

11. In which Microsoft Teams project management process group is the detailed Microsoft Teams project budget created?

12. Who is performing the work of the Microsoft Teams project?

13. Are the Microsoft Teams project team and stakeholders meeting regularly and using a meeting

agenda and taking notes to accurately document what is being covered and what happened in the weekly meetings?

14. Just how important is your work to the overall success of the Microsoft Teams project?

15. Are stakeholders properly informed about the status of the Microsoft Teams project?

16. What business situation is being addressed?

17. Professionals want to know what is expected from them what are the deliverables?

18. Were sponsors and decision makers available when needed outside regularly scheduled meetings?

19. Have you evaluated the teams performance and asked for feedback?

20. Will the Microsoft Teams project meet the client requirements, and will it achieve the business success criteria that justified doing the Microsoft Teams project in the first place?

1.1 Project Charter: Microsoft Teams

21. What are you striving to accomplish (measurable goal(s))?

22. Who will take notes, document decisions?

23. Why do you manage integration?

24. Where and how does the team fit within your organization structure?

25. When is a charter needed?

26. Fit with other Products Compliments – Cannibalizes?

27. How high should you set your goals?

28. Who manages integration?

29. Microsoft Teams project background: what is the primary motivation for this Microsoft Teams project?

30. Why executive support?

31. What barriers do you predict to your success?

32. Who is the sponsor?

33. What ideas do you have for initial tests of change (PDSA cycles)?

34. What date will the task finish?

35. How much?

36. What are the known stakeholder requirements?

37. What outcome, in measureable terms, are you hoping to accomplish?

38. What is the justification?

39. Customer benefits: what customer requirements does this Microsoft Teams project address?

40. Is it an improvement over existing products?

1.2 Stakeholder Register: Microsoft Teams

41. What are the major Microsoft Teams project milestones requiring communications or providing communications opportunities?

42. Who wants to talk about Security?

43. What & Why?

44. Who are the stakeholders?

45. How much influence do they have on the Microsoft Teams project?

46. How big is the gap?

47. Who is managing stakeholder engagement?

48. What opportunities exist to provide communications?

49. Is your organization ready for change?

50. What is the power of the stakeholder?

51. How should employers make voices heard?

52. How will reports be created?

1.3 Stakeholder Analysis Matrix: Microsoft Teams

53. What is relationship with the Microsoft Teams project?

54. Seasonality, weather effects?

55. How to involve media?

56. Who will be affected by the work?

57. Who holds positions of responsibility in interested organizations?

58. Sustainable financial backing?

59. Are there different rules or organizational models for men and women?

60. Partnerships, agencies, distribution?

61. Information and research?

62. What is your Risk Management?

63. Competitor intentions - various?

64. Environmental effects?

65. Why is it important to identify them?

66. Will the impacts be local, national or international?

67. Are you working on the right risks?

68. How does the Microsoft Teams project involve consultations or collaboration with other organizations?

69. Processes, systems, it, communications?

70. Do recommendations include actions to address any differential distribution of impacts?

71. Industry or lifestyle trends?

72. How to measure the achievement of the Outputs?

2.0 Planning Process Group: Microsoft Teams

73. Have more efficient (sensitive) and appropriate measures been adopted to respond to the political and socio-cultural problems identified?

74. How are it Microsoft Teams projects different?

75. Does it make any difference if you are successful?

76. Are the necessary foundations in place to ensure the sustainability of the results of the Microsoft Teams project?

77. If task x starts two days late, what is the effect on the Microsoft Teams project end date?

78. How will you do it?

79. Have operating capacities been created and/or reinforced in partners?

80. Are you just doing busywork to pass the time?

81. To what extent do the intervention objectives and strategies of the Microsoft Teams project respond to your organizations plans?

82. If action is called for, what form should it take?

83. Contingency planning. if a risk event occurs, what will you do?

84. If a risk event occurs, what will you do?

85. What is a Software Development Life Cycle (SDLC)?

86. Why do it Microsoft Teams projects fail?

87. How does activity resource estimation affect activity duration estimation?

88. How can you make your needs known?

89. In which Microsoft Teams project management process group is the detailed Microsoft Teams project budget created?

90. To what extent are the visions and actions of the partners consistent or divergent with regard to the program?

2.1 Project Management Plan: Microsoft Teams

91. What went right?

92. Do the proposed changes from the Microsoft Teams project include any significant risks to safety?

93. What would you do differently?

94. Are there non-structural buyout or relocation recommendations?

95. How can you best help your organization to develop consistent practices in Microsoft Teams project management planning stages?

96. How do you manage integration?

97. Did the planning effort collaborate to develop solutions that integrate expertise, policies, programs, and Microsoft Teams projects across entities?

98. Was the peer (technical) review of the cost estimates duly coordinated with the cost estimate center of expertise and addressed in the review documentation and certification?

99. What data/reports/tools/etc. do your PMs need?

100. What does management expect of PMs?

101. What are the assumptions?

102. What would you do differently what did not work?

103. Where does all this information come from?

104. Will you add a schedule and diagram?

105. Does the implementation plan have an appropriate division of responsibilities?

106. Do there need to be organizational changes?

107. If the Microsoft Teams project management plan is a comprehensive document that guides you in Microsoft Teams project execution and control, then what should it NOT contain?

2.2 Scope Management Plan: Microsoft Teams

108. Has your organization done similar tasks before?

109. Timeline and milestones?

110. What if you do not have more detailed information on the report?

111. Describe the process for rejecting the Microsoft Teams project deliverables. What happens to rejected deliverables?

112. Can each item be appropriately scheduled?

113. Are there procedures in place to effectively manage interdependencies with other Microsoft Teams projects, systems, Vendors and your organizations work effort?

114. Have Microsoft Teams project success criteria been defined?

115. Would the Microsoft Teams project cost sharing involve reimbursement to the sponsor?

116. Is there an onboarding process in place?

117. Are calculations and results of analyzes essentially correct?

118. Has allowance been made for vacations, holidays,

training (learning time for each team member), staff promotions & staff turnovers?

119. Is there general agreement & acceptance of the current status and progress of the Microsoft Teams project?

120. Has a capability assessment been conducted?

121. Are Microsoft Teams project team members committed fulltime?

122. Do you have the reasons why the changes to your organizational systems and capabilities are required?

123. Materials available for performing the work?

124. Are there any windfall benefits that would accrue to the Microsoft Teams project sponsor or other parties?

125. Does the quality assurance process provide objective verification of adherence to applicable standards, procedures & requirements?

126. Are meeting minutes captured and sent out after the meeting?

127. Are tasks tracked by hours?

2.3 Requirements Management Plan: Microsoft Teams

128. How do you know that you have done this right?

129. Is stakeholder risk tolerance an important factor for the requirements process in this Microsoft Teams project?

130. Do you expect stakeholders to be cooperative?

131. How will the requirements become prioritized?

132. Do you really need to write this document at all?

133. Could inaccurate or incomplete requirements in this Microsoft Teams project create a serious risk for the business?

134. Do you have price sheets and a methodology for determining the total proposal cost?

135. Who came up with this requirement?

136. Define the help desk model. who will take full responsibility?

137. How knowledgeable is the team in the proposed application area?

138. Who will finally present the work or product(s) for acceptance?

139. Who will approve the requirements (and if multiple approvers, in what order)?

140. Do you know which stakeholders will participate in the requirements effort?

141. In case of software development; Should you have a test for each code module?

142. Have stakeholders been instructed in the Change Control process?

143. How will unresolved questions be handled once approval has been obtained?

144. Business analysis scope?

145. Did you distinguish the scope of work the contractor(s) will be required to do?

146. Will the Microsoft Teams project requirements become approved in writing?

147. What performance metrics will be used?

2.4 Requirements Documentation: Microsoft Teams

148. Can you check system requirements?

149. Do technical resources exist?

150. Does your organization restrict technical alternatives?

151. What are the attributes of a customer?

152. What are current process problems?

153. Basic work/business process; high-level, what is being touched?

154. Does the system provide the functions which best support the customers needs?

155. What is the risk associated with cost and schedule?

156. What is effective documentation?

157. What happens when requirements are wrong?

158. What will be the integration problems?

159. Are all functions required by the customer included?

160. Do your constraints stand?

161. How do you get the user to tell you what they want?

162. What facilities must be supported by the system?

163. How does what is being described meet the business need?

164. What is a show stopper in the requirements?

165. How to document system requirements?

166. Is new technology needed?

167. Where do you define what is a customer, what are the attributes of customer?

2.5 Requirements Traceability Matrix: Microsoft Teams

168. Describe the process for approving requirements so they can be added to the traceability matrix and Microsoft Teams project work can be performed. Will the Microsoft Teams project requirements become approved in writing?

169. What percentage of Microsoft Teams projects are producing traceability matrices between requirements and other work products?

170. How will it affect the stakeholders personally in their career?

171. Will you use a Requirements Traceability Matrix?

172. Why do you manage scope?

173. How do you manage scope?

174. Is there a requirements traceability process in place?

175. Do you have a clear understanding of all subcontracts in place?

176. What is the WBS?

177. How small is small enough?

178. What are the chronologies, contingencies,

consequences, criteria?

179. Why use a WBS?

2.6 Project Scope Statement: Microsoft Teams

180. Have you been able to easily identify success criteria and create objective measurements for each of the Microsoft Teams project scopes goal statements?

181. Has a method and process for requirement tracking been developed?

182. Is your organization structure appropriate for the Microsoft Teams projects size and complexity?

183. Are there backup strategies for key members of the Microsoft Teams project?

184. Is the plan for Microsoft Teams project resources adequate?

185. Is the Microsoft Teams project manager qualified and experienced in Microsoft Teams project management?

186. Is there a baseline plan against which to measure progress?

187. Was planning completed before the Microsoft Teams project was initiated?

188. Write a brief purpose statement for this Microsoft Teams project. Include a business justification statement. What is the product of this Microsoft

Teams project?

189. Which risks does the Microsoft Teams project focus on?

190. Any new risks introduced or old risks impacted. Are there issues that could affect the existing requirements for the result, service, or product if the scope changes?

191. How often do you estimate that the scope might change, and why?

192. Are the meetings set up to have assigned note takers that will add action/issues to the issue list?

193. Will the Microsoft Teams project risks be managed according to the Microsoft Teams projects risk management process?

194. Did your Microsoft Teams project ask for this?

195. Do you anticipate new stakeholders joining the Microsoft Teams project over time?

196. Will statistics related to QA be collected, trends analyzed, and problems raised as issues?

197. Elements of scope management that deal with concept development ?

198. If you were to write a list of what should not be included in the scope statement, what are the things that you would recommend be described as out-of-scope?

2.7 Assumption and Constraint Log: Microsoft Teams

199. Are there processes in place to ensure internal consistency between the source code components?

200. Is there documentation of system capability requirements, data requirements, environment requirements, security requirements, and computer and hardware requirements?

201. What other teams / processes would be impacted by changes to the current process, and how?

202. After observing execution of process, is it in compliance with the documented Plan?

203. Contradictory information between different documents?

204. What to do at recovery?

205. Have all involved stakeholders and work groups committed to the Microsoft Teams project?

206. Do documented requirements exist for all critical components and areas, including technical, business, interfaces, performance, security and conversion requirements?

207. Is the steering committee active in Microsoft Teams project oversight?

208. Does the plan conform to standards?

209. Are there nonconformance issues?

210. Have the scope, objectives, costs, benefits and impacts been communicated to all involved and/or impacted stakeholders and work groups?

211. Are there ways to reduce the time it takes to get something approved?

212. Are formal code reviews conducted?

213. Does the Microsoft Teams project have a formal Microsoft Teams project Plan?

214. Is there adequate stakeholder participation for the vetting of requirements definition, changes and management?

215. Are requirements management tracking tools and procedures in place?

216. Can the requirements be traced to the appropriate components of the solution, as well as test scripts?

217. Are funding and staffing resource estimates sufficiently detailed and documented for use in planning and tracking the Microsoft Teams project?

218. Is staff trained on the software technologies that are being used on the Microsoft Teams project?

2.8 Work Breakdown Structure: Microsoft Teams

219. Can you make it?

220. Do you need another level?

221. Who has to do it?

222. Why would you develop a Work Breakdown Structure?

223. What has to be done?

224. Why is it useful?

225. How big is a work-package?

226. How far down?

227. How much detail?

228. How will you and your Microsoft Teams project team define the Microsoft Teams projects scope and work breakdown structure?

229. When do you stop?

230. Is it a change in scope?

231. Where does it take place?

232. Is the work breakdown structure (wbs) defined

and is the scope of the Microsoft Teams project clear with assigned deliverable owners?

233. Is it still viable?

234. What is the probability of completing the Microsoft Teams project in less that xx days?

235. When does it have to be done?

236. When would you develop a Work Breakdown Structure?

237. How many levels?

238. What is the probability that the Microsoft Teams project duration will exceed xx weeks?

2.9 WBS Dictionary: Microsoft Teams

239. Are detailed work packages planned as far in advance as practicable?

240. Time-phased control account budgets?

241. Does the contractor have procedures which permit identification of recurring or non-recurring costs as necessary?

242. Is the work done on a work package level as described in the WBS dictionary?

243. Are the contractors estimates of costs at completion reconcilable with cost data reported to us?

244. Are procedures in existence that control replanning of unopened work packages, and are corresponding procedures adhered to?

245. Is work progressively subdivided into detailed work packages as requirements are defined?

246. Does the accounting system provide a basis for auditing records of direct costs chargeable to the contract?

247. Are indirect costs accumulated for comparison with the corresponding budgets?

248. Are work packages assigned to performing organizations?

249. Are data elements reconcilable between internal summary reports and reports forwarded to us?

250. Where learning is used in developing underlying budgets is there a direct relationship between anticipated learning and time phased budgets?

251. Are indirect costs charged to the appropriate indirect pools and incurring organization?

252. Are all affected work authorizations, budgeting, and scheduling documents amended to properly reflect the effects of authorized changes?

253. Are meaningful indicators identified for use in measuring the status of cost and schedule performance?

254. Intermediate schedules, as required, which provide a logical sequence from the master schedule to the control account level?

255. Are direct or indirect cost adjustments being accomplished according to accounting procedures acceptable to us?

256. Does the contractors system identify work accomplishment against the schedule plan?

257. Does the contractors system include procedures for measuring performance of the lowest level organization responsible for the control account?

258. Are estimates of costs at completion generated in a rational, consistent manner?

2.10 Schedule Management Plan: Microsoft Teams

259. Have all necessary approvals been obtained?

260. Are the activity durations realistic and at an appropriate level of detail for effective management?

261. Is an industry recognized mechanized support tool(s) being used for Microsoft Teams project scheduling & tracking?

262. Where is the scheduling tool and who has access to it to view it?

263. Does a documented Microsoft Teams project organizational policy & plan (i.e. governance model) exist?

264. Is the assigned Microsoft Teams project manager a PMP (Certified Microsoft Teams project manager) and experienced?

265. Have the key elements of a coherent Microsoft Teams project management strategy been established?

266. Are written status reports provided on a designated frequent basis?

267. Have Microsoft Teams project team accountabilities & responsibilities been clearly defined?

268. Are target dates established for each milestone deliverable?

269. Who is responsible for estimating the activity durations?

270. Can be realistically shortened (the duration of subsequent tasks)?

271. Are actuals compared against estimates to analyze and correct variances?

272. Microsoft Teams project definition & scope?

273. List all schedule constraints here. Must the Microsoft Teams project be complete by a specified date?

274. Are post milestone Microsoft Teams project reviews (PMPR) conducted with your organization at least once a year?

275. Is pert / critical path or equivalent methodology being used?

276. Does the detailed work plan match the complexity of tasks with the capabilities of personnel?

277. Have Microsoft Teams project management standards and procedures been identified / established and documented?

2.11 Activity List: Microsoft Teams

278. In what sequence?

279. How difficult will it be to do specific activities on this Microsoft Teams project?

280. What is your organizations history in doing similar activities?

281. Are the required resources available or need to be acquired?

282. Is there anything planned that does not need to be here?

283. What are the critical bottleneck activities?

284. Can you determine the activity that must finish, before this activity can start?

285. Where will it be performed?

286. Is infrastructure setup part of your Microsoft Teams project?

287. How detailed should a Microsoft Teams project get?

288. How can the Microsoft Teams project be displayed graphically to better visualize the activities?

289. How much slack is available in the Microsoft Teams project?

290. What will be performed?

291. How should ongoing costs be monitored to try to keep the Microsoft Teams project within budget?

292. Who will perform the work?

293. How will it be performed?

294. When will the work be performed?

295. What is the total time required to complete the Microsoft Teams project if no delays occur?

296. What went wrong?

2.12 Activity Attributes: Microsoft Teams

297. Would you consider either of corresponding activities an outlier?

298. How do you manage time?

299. Have you identified the Activity Leveling Priority code value on each activity?

300. Are the required resources available?

301. Time for overtime?

302. Can more resources be added?

303. What is the general pattern here?

304. Which method produces the more accurate cost assignment?

305. How much activity detail is required?

306. Were there other ways you could have organized the data to achieve similar results?

307. Activity: fair or not fair?

308. What is missing?

309. Do you feel very comfortable with your prediction?

310. Resource is assigned to?

311. Where else does it apply?

312. Is there a trend during the year?

2.13 Milestone List: Microsoft Teams

313. Which path is the critical path?

314. Competitive advantages?

315. Who will manage the Microsoft Teams project on a day-to-day basis?

316. What would happen if a delivery of material was one week late?

317. How late can each activity be finished and started?

318. How difficult will it be to do specific activities on this Microsoft Teams project?

319. Sustaining internal capabilities?

320. Identify critical paths (one or more) and which activities are on the critical path?

321. How will the milestone be verified?

322. Usps (unique selling points)?

323. Describe your organizations strengths and core competencies. What factors will make your organization succeed?

324. Calculate how long can activity be delayed?

325. What specific improvements did you make to the

Microsoft Teams project proposal since the previous time?

326. How soon can the activity finish?

327. Describe the concept of the technology, product or service that will be or has been developed. How will it be used?

328. Vital contracts and partners?

329. How late can the activity start?

330. What has been done so far?

331. How late can the activity finish?

2.14 Network Diagram: Microsoft Teams

332. What is the completion time?

333. What are the tools?

334. Which type of network diagram allows you to depict four types of dependencies?

335. What job or jobs precede it?

336. What is the lowest cost to complete this Microsoft Teams project in xx weeks?

337. If x is long, what would be the completion time if you break x into two parallel parts of y weeks and z weeks?

338. If a current contract exists, can you provide the vendor name, contract start, and contract expiration date?

339. Are you on time?

340. Are the gantt chart and/or network diagram updated periodically and used to assess the overall Microsoft Teams project timetable?

341. What are the Key Success Factors?

342. What to do and When?

343. If the Microsoft Teams project network diagram cannot change and you have extra personnel resources, what is the BEST thing to do?

344. What activity must be completed immediately before this activity can start?

345. What activities must occur simultaneously with this activity?

346. Planning: who, how long, what to do?

347. What activities must follow this activity?

348. Why must you schedule milestones, such as reviews, throughout the Microsoft Teams project?

349. What must be completed before an activity can be started?

350. Can you calculate the confidence level?

2.15 Activity Resource Requirements: Microsoft Teams

351. When does monitoring begin?

352. Anything else?

353. Which logical relationship does the PDM use most often?

354. Do you use tools like decomposition and rolling-wave planning to produce the activity list and other outputs?

355. Why do you do that?

356. How do you handle petty cash?

357. How many signatures do you require on a check and does this match what is in your policy and procedures?

358. Other support in specific areas?

359. What are constraints that you might find during the Human Resource Planning process?

360. What is the Work Plan Standard?

361. Are there unresolved issues that need to be addressed?

362. Organizational Applicability?

2.16 Resource Breakdown Structure: Microsoft Teams

363. What is the purpose of assigning and documenting responsibility?

364. Is predictive resource analysis being done?

365. How difficult will it be to do specific activities on this Microsoft Teams project?

366. What defines a successful Microsoft Teams project?

367. What is the difference between % Complete and % work?

368. Why do you do it?

369. Who delivers the information?

370. What is Microsoft Teams project communication management?

371. Who will be used as a Microsoft Teams project team member?

372. What are the requirements for resource data?

373. Who will use the system?

374. Who needs what information?

375. Which resources should be in the resource pool?

2.17 Activity Duration Estimates: Microsoft Teams

376. Is action taken to increase the effectiveness and efficiency of Microsoft Teams projects?

377. Will additional funds be needed for hardware or software?

378. What are the typical challenges Microsoft Teams project teams face during each of the five process groups?

379. How difficult will it be to complete specific activities on this Microsoft Teams project?

380. Are Microsoft Teams project records organized, maintained, and assessable by Microsoft Teams project team members?

381. What do you think about the WBSs for them?

382. What type of people would you want on your team?

383. What are the key components of a Microsoft Teams project communications plan?

384. What are the Microsoft Teams project management deliverables of each process group?

385. Will it help promote wellness at your organization and reduce insurance costs?

386. What do you think the real problem was in this case?

387. Is a contract change control system defined to manage changes to contract terms and conditions?

388. If you plan to take the PMP exam soon, what should you do to prepare?

389. Which suggestions do you find most useful?

390. What tasks can take place concurrently?

391. What are some crucial elements of a good Microsoft Teams project plan?

392. Is a Microsoft Teams project charter created once a Microsoft Teams project is formally recognized?

393. Who will promote it?

394. Are tools and techniques defined for gathering, integrating and distributing Microsoft Teams project outputs?

395. Calculate the expected duration for an activity that has a most likely time of 5, a pessimistic time of 13, and a optimiztic time of 3?

2.18 Duration Estimating Worksheet: Microsoft Teams

396. When, then?

397. When does your organization expect to be able to complete it?

398. Science = process: remember the scientific method?

399. How should ongoing costs be monitored to try to keep the Microsoft Teams project within budget?

400. Does the Microsoft Teams project provide innovative ways for stakeholders to overcome obstacles or deliver better outcomes?

401. Why estimate costs?

402. Define the work as completely as possible. What work will be included in the Microsoft Teams project?

403. Do any colleagues have experience with your organization and/or RFPs?

404. Small or large Microsoft Teams project?

405. Done before proceeding with this activity or what can be done concurrently?

406. What is an Average Microsoft Teams project?

407. What is the total time required to complete the Microsoft Teams project if no delays occur?

408. How can the Microsoft Teams project be displayed graphically to better visualize the activities?

409. Is the Microsoft Teams project responsive to community need?

410. Why estimate time and cost?

411. Is this operation cost effective?

412. Is a construction detail attached (to aid in explanation)?

413. What is cost and Microsoft Teams project cost management?

414. What questions do you have?

2.19 Project Schedule: Microsoft Teams

415. What is the difference?

416. It allows the Microsoft Teams project to be delivered on schedule. How Do you Use Schedules?

417. Verify that the update is accurate. Are all remaining durations correct?

418. What is risk management?

419. Why do you need to manage Microsoft Teams project Risk?

420. Is the structure for tracking the Microsoft Teams project schedule well defined and assigned to a specific individual?

421. Why or why not?

422. If you can not fix it, how do you do it differently?

423. Is Microsoft Teams project work proceeding in accordance with the original Microsoft Teams project schedule?

424. How do you use schedules?

425. How closely did the initial Microsoft Teams project Schedule compare with the actual schedule?

426. Should you have a test for each code module?

427. Why is this particularly bad?

428. Why do you need schedules?

429. How do you know that youhave done this right?

430. Are procedures defined by which the Microsoft Teams project schedule may be changed?

431. Understand the constraints used in preparing the schedule. Are activities connected because logic dictates the order in which others occur?

432. Are activities connected because logic dictates the order in which others occur?

2.20 Cost Management Plan: Microsoft Teams

433. Are adequate resources provided for the quality assurance function?

434. Is there a Steering Committee in place?

435. Does all Microsoft Teams project documentation reside in a common repository for easy access?

436. Are there checklists created to determine if all quality processes are followed?

437. What is Microsoft Teams project management?

438. Are key risk mitigation strategies added to the Microsoft Teams project schedule?

439. Are all resource assumptions documented?

440. Has Microsoft Teams project success criteria been defined?

441. Have all documents been archived in a Microsoft Teams project repository for each release?

442. Have stakeholder accountabilities & responsibilities been clearly defined?

443. Have the key functions and capabilities been defined and assigned to each release or iteration?

444. Is the Microsoft Teams project schedule available for all Microsoft Teams project team members to review?

445. Sensitivity analysis?

446. Have the reasons why the changes to your organizational systems and capabilities are required?

447. Does the Microsoft Teams project have a formal Microsoft Teams project Charter?

448. Does the Microsoft Teams project have a Statement of Work?

449. Are change requests logged and managed?

450. Are assumptions being identified, recorded, analyzed, qualified and closed?

451. The definition of the Microsoft Teams project scope what needs to be accomplished?

2.21 Activity Cost Estimates: Microsoft Teams

452. Were decisions made in a timely manner?

453. The impact and what actions were taken?

454. What happens if you cannot produce the documentation for the single audit?

455. What is the activity inventory?

456. Is costing method consistent with study goals?

457. What were things that you need to improve?

458. What makes a good activity description?

459. What are the audit requirements?

460. Which contract type places the most risk on the seller?

461. What communication items need improvement?

462. Does the estimator have experience?

463. What are you looking for?

464. Will you need to provide essential services information about activities?

465. What is the Microsoft Teams projects

sustainability strategy that will ensure Microsoft Teams project results will endure or be sustained?

466. How do you do activity recasts?

467. Measurable - are the targets measurable?

468. Where can you get activity reports?

469. How do you fund change orders?

470. Were you satisfied with the work?

2.22 Cost Estimating Worksheet: Microsoft Teams

471. Who is best positioned to know and assist in identifying corresponding factors?

472. Value pocket identification & quantification what are value pockets?

473. What is the estimated labor cost today based upon this information?

474. Identify the timeframe necessary to monitor progress and collect data to determine how the selected measure has changed?

475. How will the results be shared and to whom?

476. Is the Microsoft Teams project responsive to community need?

477. What additional Microsoft Teams project(s) could be initiated as a result of this Microsoft Teams project?

478. Can a trend be established from historical performance data on the selected measure and are the criteria for using trend analysis or forecasting methods met?

479. What costs are to be estimated?

480. Is it feasible to establish a control group arrangement?

481. What info is needed?

482. What is the purpose of estimating?

483. Does the Microsoft Teams project provide innovative ways for stakeholders to overcome obstacles or deliver better outcomes?

484. What will others want?

485. What can be included?

486. What happens to any remaining funds not used?

487. Ask: are others positioned to know, are others credible, and will others cooperate?

488. Will the Microsoft Teams project collaborate with the local community and leverage resources?

2.23 Cost Baseline: Microsoft Teams

489. Are you meeting with your team regularly?

490. What do you want to measure ?

491. How fast?

492. Pcs for your new business. what would the life cycle costs be?

493. Have you identified skills that are missing from your team?

494. Has the appropriate access to relevant data and analysis capability been granted?

495. Are procedures defined by which the cost baseline may be changed?

496. Is request in line with priorities?

497. Have the actual milestone completion dates been compared to the approved schedule?

498. Has the actual cost of the Microsoft Teams project (or Microsoft Teams project phase) been tallied and compared to the approved budget?

499. How will cost estimates be used?

500. Does the suggested change request seem to represent a necessary enhancement to the product?

501. Has operations management formally accepted responsibility for operating and maintaining the product(s) or service(s) delivered by the Microsoft Teams project?

502. Is the requested change request a result of changes in other Microsoft Teams project(s)?

503. Has the Microsoft Teams projected annual cost to operate and maintain the product(s) or service(s) been approved and funded?

504. Has the Microsoft Teams project documentation been archived or otherwise disposed as described in the Microsoft Teams project communication plan?

505. Microsoft Teams project goals -should others be reconsidered?

506. What is the consequence?

507. Is there anything you need from upper management in order to be successful?

2.24 Quality Management Plan: Microsoft Teams

508. What would you gain if you spent time working to improve this process?

509. Have all involved stakeholders and work groups committed to the Microsoft Teams project?

510. How does the material compare to a regulatory threshold?

511. Was trending evident between reviews?

512. What worked well?

513. What is the Difference Between a QMP and QAPP?

514. What are the established criteria that sampling / testing data are compared against?

515. What process do you use to minimize errors, defects, and rework?

516. Were there any deficiencies / issues in prior years self-assessment?

517. Would impacts defined serve as impediments?

518. What key performance indicators does your organization use to measure, manage, and improve key processes?

519. Does the Microsoft Teams project have a formal Microsoft Teams project Plan?

520. How are people conducting sampling trained?

521. How do you prioritize?

522. How are senior leaders, employees, and your organization involved in supporting the community?

523. What are the appropriate test methods to be used?

524. Is there a procedure for this process?

525. How is equipment calibrated?

2.25 Quality Metrics: Microsoft Teams

526. What makes a visualization memorable?

527. Can you correlate your quality metrics to profitability?

528. How do you know if everyone is trying to improve the right things?

529. Were quality attributes reported?

530. What can manufacturing professionals do to ensure quality is seen as an integral part of the entire product lifecycle?

531. How do you calculate corresponding metrics?

532. What documentation is required?

533. There are many reasons to shore up quality-related metrics, and what metrics are important?

534. Are applicable standards referenced and available?

535. Has trace of defects been initiated?

536. Have risk areas been identified?

537. When is the security analysis testing complete?

538. Who notifies stakeholders of normal and abnormal results?

539. Where did complaints, returns and warranty claims come from?

540. Do you know how much profit a 10% decrease in waste would generate?

541. What does this tell us?

542. What is the benchmark?

543. What method of measurement do you use?

544. Is quality culture a competitive advantage?

545. What group is empowered to define quality requirements?

2.26 Process Improvement Plan: Microsoft Teams

546. What is the return on investment?

547. What is quality and how will you ensure it?

548. What personnel are the sponsors for that initiative?

549. Modeling current processes is great, and will you ever see a return on that investment?

550. The motive is determined by asking, Why do you want to achieve this goal?

551. Management commitment at all levels?

552. What personnel are the coaches for your initiative?

553. Does explicit definition of the measures exist?

554. What actions are needed to address the problems and achieve the goals?

555. Where are you now?

556. Are you meeting the quality standards?

557. Who should prepare the process improvement action plan?

558. What personnel are the champions for the initiative?

559. Are you making progress on the improvement framework?

560. If a process improvement framework is being used, which elements will help the problems and goals listed?

561. Has a process guide to collect the data been developed?

562. Does your process ensure quality?

563. Why do you want to achieve the goal?

564. Where do you want to be?

565. How do you manage quality?

2.27 Responsibility Assignment Matrix: Microsoft Teams

566. The already stated responsible for overhead performance control of related costs?

567. Can the contractor substantiate work package and planning package budgets?

568. Does the contractors system include procedures for measuring the performance of critical subcontractors?

569. Too many as: does a proper segregation of duties exist?

570. Do all the identified groups or people really need to be consulted?

571. Is the entire contract planned in time-phased control accounts to the extent practicable?

572. Does the contractor use objective results, design reviews and tests to trace schedule performance?

573. What will the work cost?

574. How do you assist them to be as productive as possible?

575. The anticipated business volume?

576. How can this help you with team building?

577. What simple tool can you use to help identify and prioritize Microsoft Teams project risks that is very low tech and high touch?

578. Are the wbs and organizational levels for application of the Microsoft Teams projected overhead costs identified?

579. What expertise is available in your department?

580. Do work packages consist of discrete tasks which are adequately described?

581. Contract line items and end items?

582. Is all contract work included in the CWBS?

583. Is work properly classified as measured effort, LOE, or apportioned effort and appropriately separated?

584. Do you need to convince people that its well worth the time and effort?

2.28 Roles and Responsibilities: Microsoft Teams

585. Concern: where are you limited or have no authority, where you can not influence?

586. What should you do now to ensure that you are exceeding expectations and excelling in your current position?

587. Does the team have access to and ability to use data analysis tools?

588. Was the expectation clearly communicated?

589. Where are you most strong as a supervisor?

590. Influence: what areas of organizational decision making are you able to influence when you do not have authority to make the final decision?

591. Attainable / achievable: the goal is attainable; can you actually accomplish the goal?

592. Key conclusions and recommendations: Are conclusions and recommendations relevant and acceptable?

593. Are your policies supportive of a culture of quality data?

594. What expectations were met?

595. Do you take the time to clearly define roles and responsibilities on Microsoft Teams project tasks?

596. What areas of supervision are challenging for you?

597. Are the quality assurance functions and related roles and responsibilities clearly defined?

598. What should you highlight for improvement?

599. Once the responsibilities are defined for the Microsoft Teams project, have the deliverables, roles and responsibilities been clearly communicated to every participant?

600. Once the responsibilities are defined for the Microsoft Teams project, have the deliverables, roles and responsibilities been clearly communicated to every participant?

601. What are your major roles and responsibilities in the area of performance measurement and assessment?

602. Authority: what areas/Microsoft Teams projects in your work do you have the authority to decide upon and act on the already stated decisions?

603. Do the values and practices inherent in the culture of your organization foster or hinder the process?

604. Is feedback clearly communicated and non-judgmental?

2.29 Human Resource Management Plan: Microsoft Teams

605. Were Microsoft Teams project team members involved in the development of activity & task decomposition?

606. Are Microsoft Teams project contact logs kept up to date?

607. Is the Microsoft Teams project schedule available for all Microsoft Teams project team members to review?

608. What skills, knowledge and experiences are required?

609. Are the key elements of a Microsoft Teams project Charter present?

610. Have all documents been archived in a Microsoft Teams project repository for each release?

611. Are risk oriented checklists used during risk identification?

612. Are all vendor contracts closed out?

613. Has the budget been baselined?

614. Have Microsoft Teams project team accountabilities & responsibilities been clearly defined?

615. Have all unresolved risks been documented?

616. What is this Microsoft Teams project aiming to achieve?

617. Are meeting objectives identified for each meeting?

618. What areas does the group agree are the biggest success on the Microsoft Teams project?

619. Is a stakeholder management plan in place that covers topics?

620. Are all payments made according to the contract(s)?

621. Are procurement deliverables arriving on time and to specification?

622. How complete is the human resource management plan?

623. Has the scope management document been updated and distributed to help prevent scope creep?

2.30 Communications Management Plan: Microsoft Teams

624. Why is stakeholder engagement important?

625. What steps can you take for a positive relationship?

626. Who needs to know and how much?

627. Do you ask; can you recommend others for you to talk with about this initiative?

628. What data is going to be required?

629. Is the stakeholder role recognized by your organization?

630. Who will use or be affected by the result of a Microsoft Teams project?

631. Are the stakeholders getting the information others need, are others consulted, are concerns addressed?

632. How were corresponding initiatives successful?

633. Are stakeholders internal or external?

634. How often do you engage with stakeholders?

635. What is the stakeholders level of authority?

636. Who were proponents/opponents?

637. Who to share with?

638. Do you then often overlook a key stakeholder or stakeholder group?

639. What approaches do you use?

640. Are others part of the communications management plan?

641. Who is the stakeholder?

642. Who are the members of the governing body?

643. How did the term stakeholder originate?

2.31 Risk Management Plan: Microsoft Teams

644. Are the required plans included, such as nonstructural flood risk management plans?

645. Anticipated volatility of the requirements?

646. Do the requirements require the creation of components that are unlike anything your organization has previously built?

647. What is the impact to the Microsoft Teams project if the item is not resolved in a timely fashion?

648. Risk documentation: what reporting formats and processes will be used for risk management activities?

649. Was an original risk assessment/risk management plan completed?

650. Are the metrics meaningful and useful?

651. Have you worked with the customer in the past?

652. What did not work so well?

653. What are the chances the event will occur?

654. How can the process be made more effective or less cumbersome (process improvements)?

655. Is the process being followed?

656. Do requirements demand the use of new analysis, design, or testing methods?

657. How risk averse are you?

658. Are enough people available?

659. Is the number of people on the Microsoft Teams project team adequate to do the job?

660. Have staff received necessary training?

661. Litigation – what is the probability that lawsuits will cause problems or delays in the Microsoft Teams project?

662. Do the people have the right combinations of skills?

663. Risk categories: what are the main categories of risks that should be addressed on this Microsoft Teams project?

2.32 Risk Register: Microsoft Teams

664. Assume the event happens, what is the Most Likely impact?

665. What are your key risks/show istoppers and what is being done to manage them?

666. Are there any gaps in the evidence?

667. Who is going to do it?

668. Are implemented controls working as others should?

669. Risk probability and impact: how will the probabilities and impacts of risk items be assessed?

670. Manageability – have mitigations to the risk been identified?

671. What further options might be available for responding to the risk?

672. Are your objectives at risk?

673. Are there any knock-on effects/impact on any of the other areas?

674. What is the probability and impact of the risk occurring?

675. When is it going to be done?

676. Technology risk -is the Microsoft Teams project technically feasible?

677. Contingency actions - planned actions to reduce the immediate seriousness of the risk when it does occur. What should you do when?

678. Are there other alternative controls that could be implemented?

679. What is your current and future risk profile?

680. Are corrective measures implemented as planned?

681. What is the appropriate level of risk management for this Microsoft Teams project?

682. When will it happen?

2.33 Probability and Impact Assessment: Microsoft Teams

683. Are tools for analysis and design available?

684. Can the Microsoft Teams project proceed without assuming the risk?

685. What would be the effect of slippage?

686. Who should be responsible for the monitoring and tracking of the indicators youhave identified?

687. What risks are necessary to achieve success?

688. Are the software tools integrated with each other?

689. Who should be notified of the occurrence of each of the risk indicators?

690. Which functions, departments, and activities of your organization are going to be affected?

691. Is the customer willing to commit significant time to the requirements gathering process?

692. Who will be in command to monitor and control the performance of the consortium members (consortium leader/client)?

693. What are the industrial relations prevailing in your organization?

694. What will be the impact or consequence if the risk occurs?

695. How would you assess the risk management process in the Microsoft Teams project?

696. What should be the level of difficulty in handling the technology?

697. Has something like this been done before?

698. Do you use diagramming techniques to show cause and effect?

699. How well is the risk understood?

700. What are the preparations required for facing difficulties?

701. What should be the external organizations responsibility vis-à-vis total stake in the Microsoft Teams project?

2.34 Probability and Impact Matrix: Microsoft Teams

702. What will be the likely political environment during the life of the Microsoft Teams project?

703. How is the risk management process used in practice?

704. Can it be changed quickly?

705. Brain storm – mind maps, what if?

706. During which risk management process is a determination to transfer a risk made?

707. Does the customer have a solid idea of what is required?

708. How do you manage Microsoft Teams project Risk?

709. What can you use the analyzed risks for?

710. What will be the likely political situation during the life of the Microsoft Teams project?

711. Is a software Microsoft Teams project management tool available?

712. Mandated specific features?

713. What needs to be DONE?

714. During Microsoft Teams project executing, a team member identifies a risk that is not in the risk register. What should you do?

715. Mandated delivery date?

716. What is the probability of the risk occurring?

717. While preparing your risk responses, you identify additional risks. What should you do?

718. How would you suggest monitoring for risk transition indicators?

2.35 Risk Data Sheet: Microsoft Teams

719. What are the main threats to your existence?

720. Whom do you serve (customers)?

721. What is the chance that it will happen?

722. Has the most cost-effective solution been chosen?

723. Is the data sufficiently specified in terms of the type of failure being analyzed, and its frequency or probability?

724. What is the likelihood of it happening?

725. Type of risk identified?

726. How can it happen?

727. What were the Causes that contributed?

728. What are you weak at and therefore need to do better?

729. Risk of what?

730. What was measured?

731. Do effective diagnostic tests exist?

732. Potential for recurrence?

733. What do you know?

734. What will be the consequences if it happens?

735. What is the environment within which you operate (social trends, economic, community values, broad based participation, national directions etc.)?

736. What if client refuses?

737. How can hazards be reduced?

738. Has a sensitivity analysis been carried out?

2.36 Procurement Management Plan: Microsoft Teams

739. Are all key components of a Quality Assurance Plan present?

740. Are metrics used to evaluate and manage Vendors?

741. Are decisions made in a timely manner?

742. Has the Microsoft Teams project manager been identified?

743. Financial capacity; does the seller have, or can the seller reasonably be expected to obtain, the financial resources needed?

744. Have all team members been part of identifying risks?

745. Pareto diagrams, statistical sampling, flow charting or trend analysis used quality monitoring?

746. Have external dependencies been captured in the schedule?

747. What types of contracts will be used?

748. Has the business need been clearly defined?

749. Are updated Microsoft Teams project time & resource estimates reasonable based on the current

Microsoft Teams project stage?

750. Is quality monitored from the perspective of the customers needs and expectations?

751. Is there a requirements change management processes in place?

752. Similar Microsoft Teams projects?

753. Does the Microsoft Teams project have a formal Microsoft Teams project Charter?

2.37 Source Selection Criteria: Microsoft Teams

754. What are the limitations on pre-competitive range communications?

755. What will you use to capture evaluation and subsequent documentation?

756. What does an evaluation address and what does a sample resemble?

757. In which phase of the acquisition process cycle does source qualifications reside?

758. What should a DRFP include?

759. How should comments received in response to a RFP be handled?

760. How can solicitation Schedules be improved to yield more effective price competition?

761. How do you facilitate evaluation against published criteria?

762. What information may not be provided?

763. Who should attend debriefings?

764. Is there collaboration among your evaluators?

765. What are the most critical evaluation criteria that

prove to be tiebreakers in the evaluation of proposals?

766. What benefits are accrued from issuing a DRFP in advance of issuing a final RFP?

767. Are there any specific considerations that precludes offers from being selected as the awardee?

768. What source selection software is your team using?

769. How should oral presentations be evaluated?

770. What documentation is necessary regarding electronic communications?

771. What is the role of counsel in the procurement process?

772. What should be considered?

773. Is a cost realism analysis used?

2.38 Stakeholder Management Plan: Microsoft Teams

774. What training requirements are there based upon the required skills and resources?

775. Which of the records created within the Microsoft Teams project, if any, does the Business Owner require access to?

776. When would you develop a Microsoft Teams project Business Plan?

777. Who will be collecting information?

778. Is a pmo (Microsoft Teams project management office) in place and does it provide oversight to the Microsoft Teams project?

779. Are the payment terms being followed?

780. Is the performance of the supplier to be rated and documented?

781. What are the advantages and disadvantages of using external contracted resources?

782. Are milestone deliverables effectively tracked and compared to Microsoft Teams project plan?

783. Who is responsible for the post implementation review process?

784. Are post milestone Microsoft Teams project reviews (PMPR) conducted with your organization at least once a year?

785. Does the resource management plan include a personnel development plan?

786. What is the drawback in using qualitative Microsoft Teams project selection techniques?

787. Which impacts could serve as impediments?

788. Who is responsible for arranging and managing the review(s)?

789. Are changes in scope (deliverable commitments) agreed to by all affected groups & individuals?

790. Is there a formal set of procedures supporting Issues Management?

791. Where does the information come from?

2.39 Change Management Plan: Microsoft Teams

792. What are you trying to achieve as a result of communication?

793. Have the approved procedures and policies been published?

794. What tasks are needed?

795. How do you know the requirements you documented are the right ones?

796. Is it the same for each of the business units?

797. Is there a software application relevant to this deliverable?

798. What new roles are needed?

799. Has the priority for this Microsoft Teams project been set by the Business Unit Management Team?

800. What skills, education, knowledge, or work experiences should the resources have for each identified competency?

801. How does the principle of senders and receivers make the Microsoft Teams project communications effort more complex?

802. How much change management is needed?

803. Identify the current level of skills and knowledge and behaviours of the group that will be impacted on. What prerequisite knowledge do corresponding groups need?

804. Who is the target audience of the piece of information?

805. Have the business unit contacts been selected and notified?

806. What did the people around you say about it?

807. What are the needs, priorities and special interests of the audience?

808. Are there any restrictions on who can receive the communications?

809. What policies and procedures need to be changed?

810. Who is the audience for change management activities?

3.0 Executing Process Group: Microsoft Teams

811. What are the typical Microsoft Teams project management skills?

812. What are some crucial elements of a good Microsoft Teams project plan?

813. What areas does the group agree are the biggest success on the Microsoft Teams project?

814. What is involved in the solicitation process?

815. Is the program supported by national and/or local organizations?

816. Is the Microsoft Teams project performing better or worse than planned?

817. How do you prevent staff are just doing busywork to pass the time?

818. What are the Microsoft Teams project management deliverables of each process group?

819. How can you use Microsoft Microsoft Teams project and Excel to assist in Microsoft Teams project risk management?

820. How do you enter durations, link tasks, and view critical path information?

821. What will you do to minimize the impact should a risk event occur?

822. Are the necessary foundations in place to ensure the sustainability of the results of the programme?

823. Why is it important to determine activity sequencing on Microsoft Teams projects?

824. What areas were overlooked on this Microsoft Teams project?

825. What are the critical steps involved in selecting measures and initiatives?

826. How can your organization use a weighted decision matrix to evaluate proposals as part of source selection?

827. What are the main parts of the scope statement?

828. What is the difference between using brainstorming and the Delphi technique for risk identification?

3.1 Team Member Status Report: Microsoft Teams

829. How can you make it practical?

830. Will the staff do training or is that done by a third party?

831. Is there evidence that staff is taking a more professional approach toward management of your organizations Microsoft Teams projects?

832. Does the product, good, or service already exist within your organization?

833. How much risk is involved?

834. Are the attitudes of staff regarding Microsoft Teams project work improving?

835. Are the products of your organizations Microsoft Teams projects meeting customers objectives?

836. How it is to be done?

837. The problem with Reward & Recognition Programs is that the truly deserving people all too often get left out. How can you make it practical?

838. What specific interest groups do you have in place?

839. How will resource planning be done?

840. Are your organizations Microsoft Teams projects more successful over time?

841. Do you have an Enterprise Microsoft Teams project Management Office (EPMO)?

842. Does your organization have the means (staff, money, contract, etc.) to produce or to acquire the product, good, or service?

843. What is to be done?

844. How does this product, good, or service meet the needs of the Microsoft Teams project and your organization as a whole?

845. Does every department have to have a Microsoft Teams project Manager on staff?

846. Why is it to be done?

847. When a teams productivity and success depend on collaboration and the efficient flow of information, what generally fails them?

3.2 Change Request: Microsoft Teams

848. What is the change request log?

849. Will new change requests be acknowledged in a timely manner?

850. Where do changes come from?

851. What should be regulated in a change control operating instruction?

852. Describe how modifications, enhancements, defects and/or deficiencies shall be notified (e.g. Problem Reports, Change Requests etc) and managed. Detail warranty and/or maintenance periods?

853. Will all change requests be unconditionally tracked through this process?

854. What needs to be communicated?

855. How many times must the change be modified or presented to the change control board before it is approved?

856. What mechanism is used to appraise others of changes that are made?

857. How are the measures for carrying out the change established?

858. Will all change requests and current status be

logged?

859. How can changes be graded?

860. How fast will change requests be approved?

861. What are the Impacts to your organization?

862. How is quality being addressed on the Microsoft Teams project?

863. Will this change conflict with other requirements changes (e.g., lead to conflicting operational scenarios)?

864. Has your address changed?

865. Should staff call into the helpdesk or go to the website?

866. Customer acceptance plan how will the customer verify the change has been implemented successfully?

867. For which areas does this operating procedure apply?

3.3 Change Log: Microsoft Teams

868. Is the submitted change a new change or a modification of a previously approved change?

869. How does this change affect scope?

870. Who initiated the change request?

871. When was the request submitted?

872. How does this relate to the standards developed for specific business processes?

873. Is the requested change request a result of changes in other Microsoft Teams project(s)?

874. Is the change request open, closed or pending?

875. Is this a mandatory replacement?

876. How does this change affect the timeline of the schedule?

877. Should a more thorough impact analysis be conducted?

878. Do the described changes impact on the integrity or security of the system?

879. Will the Microsoft Teams project fail if the change request is not executed?

880. When was the request approved?

881. Is the change backward compatible without limitations?

882. Does the suggested change request represent a desired enhancement to the products functionality?

883. Is the change request within Microsoft Teams project scope?

3.4 Decision Log: Microsoft Teams

884. At what point in time does loss become unacceptable?

885. What makes you different or better than others companies selling the same thing?

886. What alternatives/risks were considered?

887. How does an increasing emphasis on cost containment influence the strategies and tactics used?

888. Decision-making process; how will the team make decisions?

889. What is the line where eDiscovery ends and document review begins?

890. How do you define success?

891. Meeting purpose; why does this team meet?

892. How does provision of information, both in terms of content and presentation, influence acceptance of alternative strategies?

893. Is everything working as expected?

894. What is the average size of your matters in an applicable measurement?

895. Behaviors; what are guidelines that the team has

identified that will assist them with getting the most out of team meetings?

896. Who is the decisionmaker?

897. Which variables make a critical difference?

898. How effective is maintaining the log at facilitating organizational learning?

899. What was the rationale for the decision?

900. Does anything need to be adjusted?

901. What are the cost implications?

902. Adversarial environment. is your opponent open to a non-traditional workflow, or will it likely challenge anything you do?

903. Linked to original objective?

3.5 Quality Audit: Microsoft Teams

904. How does your organization know that its staff entrance standards are appropriately effective and constructive and being implemented consistently?

905. It is inappropriate to seek information about the Audit Panels preliminary views including questions like why do you ask that?

906. How does your organization know that its policy management system is appropriately effective and constructive?

907. How does your organization know that its systems for communicating with and among staff are appropriately effective and constructive?

908. Are the review comments incorporated?

909. How does your organization know that its security arrangements are appropriately effective and constructive?

910. How do staff know if they are doing a good job?

911. How does your organization know that it is appropriately effective and constructive in preparing its staff for organizational aspirations?

912. How is the Strategic Plan (and other plans) reviewed and revised?

913. What are the main things that hinder your ability

to do a good job?

914. Are adequate and conveniently located toilet facilities available for use by the employees?

915. Are salvageable and salvaged medical devices stored in a manner to prevent damage and/or contamination?

916. How does your organization know that its staff financial services are appropriately effective and constructive?

917. Will the evidence likely be sufficient and appropriate?

918. Are storage areas and reconditioning operations designed to prevent mix-ups and assure orderly handling of both the distressed and reconditioned devices?

919. How does your organization know that the support for its staff is appropriately effective and constructive?

920. Are all records associated with the reconditioning of a device maintained for a minimum of two years after the sale or disposal of the last device within a lot of merchandise?

921. How does your organization know that its research funding systems are appropriately effective and constructive in enabling quality research outcomes?

922. How does the organization know that its system

for maintaining and advancing the capabilities of its staff, particularly in relation to the Mission of the organization, is appropriately effective and constructive?

923. How does your organization know that its relationships with other relevant organizations are appropriately effective and constructive?

3.6 Team Directory: Microsoft Teams

924. How and in what format should information be presented?

925. Who will talk to the customer?

926. Who will write the meeting minutes and distribute?

927. How will the team handle changes?

928. Process decisions: are all start-up, turn over and close out requirements of the contract satisfied?

929. Process decisions: how well was task order work performed?

930. Process decisions: do invoice amounts match accepted work in place?

931. How does the team resolve conflicts and ensure tasks are completed?

932. Does a Microsoft Teams project team directory list all resources assigned to the Microsoft Teams project?

933. Timing: when do the effects of communication take place?

934. Who will report Microsoft Teams project status to all stakeholders?

935. Days from the time the issue is identified?

936. When does information need to be distributed?

937. Have you decided when to celebrate the Microsoft Teams projects completion date?

938. Process decisions: are there any statutory or regulatory issues relevant to the timely execution of work?

939. When will you produce deliverables?

940. How will you accomplish and manage the objectives?

941. Do purchase specifications and configurations match requirements?

942. Where should the information be distributed?

3.7 Team Operating Agreement: Microsoft Teams

943. Do you call or email participants to ensure understanding, follow-through and commitment to the meeting outcomes?

944. Reimbursements: how will the team members be reimbursed for expenses and time commitments?

945. What is teaming?

946. How will you resolve conflict efficiently and respectfully?

947. Do you begin with a question to engage everyone?

948. How do you want to be thought of and known within your organization?

949. Do you record meetings for the already stated unable to attend?

950. Must your team members rely on the expertise of other members to complete tasks?

951. Do you brief absent members after they view meeting notes or listen to a recording?

952. What is the anticipated procedure (recruitment, solicitation of volunteers, or assignment) for selecting team members?

953. Resource allocation: how will individual team members account for time and expenses, and how will this be allocated in the team budget?

954. Do you leverage technology engagement tools group chat, polls, screen sharing, etc.?

955. To whom do you deliver your services?

956. Conflict resolution: how will disputes and other conflicts be mediated or resolved?

957. What administrative supports will be put in place to support the team and the teams supervisor?

958. How will your group handle planned absences?

959. Do you prevent individuals from dominating the meeting?

960. Do you use a parking lot for any items that are important and outside of the agenda?

961. What is group supervision?

962. Why does your organization want to participate in teaming?

3.8 Team Performance Assessment: Microsoft Teams

963. To what degree will new and supplemental skills be introduced as the need is recognized?

964. Delaying market entry: how long is too long?

965. To what degree do team members agree with the goals, relative importance, and the ways in which achievement will be measured?

966. What are you doing specifically to develop the leaders around you?

967. Lack of method variance in self-reported affect and perceptions at work: Reality or artifact?

968. To what degree are fresh input and perspectives systematically caught and added (for example, through information and analysis, new members, and senior sponsors)?

969. Effects of crew composition on crew performance: Does the whole equal the sum of its parts?

970. To what degree are the skill areas critical to team performance present?

971. What are teams?

972. Individual task proficiency and team process

behavior: what is important for team functioning?

973. How do you encourage members to learn from each other?

974. To what degree can all members engage in open and interactive considerations?

975. To what degree do members understand and articulate the same purpose without relying on ambiguous abstractions?

976. To what degree can team members vigorously define the teams purpose in considerations with others who are not part of the functioning team?

977. How does Microsoft Teams project termination impact Microsoft Teams project team members?

978. To what degree can team members meet frequently enough to accomplish the teams ends?

979. To what degree can the team measure progress against specific goals?

980. To what degree will the team ensure that all members equitably share the work essential to the success of the team?

981. To what degree does the teams work approach provide opportunity for members to engage in results-based evaluation?

982. To what degree does the teams purpose contain themes that are particularly meaningful and memorable?

3.9 Team Member Performance Assessment: Microsoft Teams

983. What future plans (e.g., modifications) do you have for your program?

984. Where can team members go for more detailed information on performance measurement and assessment?

985. Does platform-specific assessment information contribute to training placement or tailoring of instruction (e.g. aptitude-treatment interaction)?

986. Can your organization rate by exception and assume that most employees are performing at an acceptable level?

987. To what degree is the team cognizant of small wins to be celebrated along the way?

988. How do you start collaborating?

989. To what degree is there a sense that only the team can succeed?

990. To what degree do team members feel that the purpose of the team is important, if not exciting?

991. How accurately is your plan implemented?

992. Does the rater (supervisor) have the authority or responsibility to tell an employee that the employees

performance is unsatisfactory?

993. How was the determination made for which training platforms would be used (i.e., media selection)?

994. To what degree do members articulate the goals beyond the team membership?

995. What are best practices in use for the performance measurement system?

996. How are assessments designed, delivered, and otherwise used to maximize training?

997. What are acceptable governance changes?

998. What does collaboration look like?

999. Who should attend?

1000. Is there reluctance to join a team?

3.10 Issue Log: Microsoft Teams

1001. How is this initiative related to other portfolios, programs, or Microsoft Teams projects?

1002. Is there an important stakeholder who is actively opposed and will not receive messages?

1003. What steps can you take for positive relationships?

1004. Are the stakeholders getting the information they need, are they consulted, are concerns addressed?

1005. What approaches to you feel are the best ones to use?

1006. What would have to change?

1007. Are there too many who have an interest in some aspect of your work?

1008. Are you constantly rushing from meeting to meeting?

1009. What is the impact on the risks?

1010. Do you feel a register helps?

1011. Do you prepare stakeholder engagement plans?

1012. What is a Stakeholder?

1013. Do you have members of your team responsible for certain stakeholders?

1014. Who do you turn to if you have questions?

1015. Can you think of other people who might have concerns or interests?

1016. Why not more evaluators?

1017. Where do team members get information?

1018. Are the Microsoft Teams project issues uniquely identified, including to which product they refer?

1019. Can an impact cause deviation beyond team, stage or Microsoft Teams project tolerances?

4.0 Monitoring and Controlling Process Group: Microsoft Teams

1020. Did you implement the program as designed?

1021. Do the partners have sufficient financial capacity to keep up the benefits produced by the programme?

1022. Is the program making progress in helping to achieve the set results?

1023. How is agile portfolio management done?

1024. How were collaborations developed, and how are they sustained?

1025. Do the products created live up to the necessary quality?

1026. How many more potential communications channels were introduced by the discovery of the new stakeholders?

1027. How was the program set-up initiated?

1028. Did the Microsoft Teams project team have the right skills?

1029. What are the deliverables?

1030. How should needs be met?

1031. What factors are contributing to progress or delay in the achievement of products and results?

1032. Do clients benefit (change) from the services?

1033. Is the verbiage used appropriate and understandable?

1034. Does the solution fit in with organizations technical architectural requirements?

1035. Based on your Microsoft Teams project communication management plan, what worked well?

4.1 Project Performance Report: Microsoft Teams

1036. To what degree are the demands of the task compatible with and converge with the relationships of the informal organization?

1037. To what degree can the cognitive capacity of individuals accommodate the flow of information?

1038. To what degree will each member have the opportunity to advance his or her professional skills in all three of the above categories while contributing to the accomplishment of the teams purpose and goals?

1039. To what degree does the teams purpose constitute a broader, deeper aspiration than just accomplishing short-term goals?

1040. To what degree do all members feel responsible for all agreed-upon measures?

1041. To what degree are the demands of the task compatible with and converge with the mission and functions of the formal organization?

1042. How is the data used?

1043. To what degree does the teams work approach provide opportunity for members to engage in open interaction?

1044. To what degree do the goals specify concrete

team work products?

1045. How will procurement be coordinated with other Microsoft Teams project aspects, such as scheduling and performance reporting?

1046. To what degree can the team ensure that all members are individually and jointly accountable for the teams purpose, goals, approach, and work-products?

1047. To what degree do team members understand one anothers roles and skills?

1048. To what degree does the informal organization make use of individual resources and meet individual needs?

1049. To what degree do team members articulate the teams work approach?

1050. To what degree are the teams goals and objectives clear, simple, and measurable?

4.2 Variance Analysis: Microsoft Teams

1051. Are data elements reconcilable between internal summary reports and reports forwarded to the stakeholders?

1052. What are the direct labor dollars and/or hours?

1053. Budget versus actual. how does the monthly budget compare to actual experience?

1054. Is there a logical explanation for any variance?

1055. Favorable or unfavorable variance?

1056. Are the bases and rates for allocating costs from each indirect pool consistently applied?

1057. What causes selling price variance?

1058. Are procedures for variance analysis documented and consistently applied at the control account level and selected WBS and organizational levels at least monthly as a routine task?

1059. What is the actual cost of work performed?

1060. Is cost and schedule performance measurement done in a consistent, systematic manner?

1061. How do you manage changes in the nature of the overhead requirements?

1062. What are the actual costs to date?

1063. There are detailed schedules which support control account and work package start and completion dates/events?

1064. At what point should variances be isolated and brought to the attention of the management?

1065. Are all cwbs elements specified for external reporting?

1066. Are records maintained to show how management reserves are used?

1067. How does the monthly budget compare to the actual experience?

4.3 Earned Value Status: Microsoft Teams

1068. If earned value management (EVM) is so good in determining the true status of a Microsoft Teams project and Microsoft Teams project its completion, why is it that hardly any one uses it in information systems related Microsoft Teams projects?

1069. How much is it going to cost by the finish?

1070. Where is evidence-based earned value in your organization reported?

1071. Earned value can be used in almost any Microsoft Teams project situation and in almost any Microsoft Teams project environment. it may be used on large Microsoft Teams projects, medium sized Microsoft Teams projects, tiny Microsoft Teams projects (in cut-down form), complex and simple Microsoft Teams projects and in any market sector. some people, of course, know all about earned value, they have used it for years - but perhaps not as effectively as they could have?

1072. Verification is a process of ensuring that the developed system satisfies the stakeholders agreements and specifications; Are you building the product right? What do you haverify?

1073. Where are your problem areas?

1074. How does this compare with other Microsoft

Teams projects?

1075. When is it going to finish?

1076. Are you hitting your Microsoft Teams projects targets?

1077. Validation is a process of ensuring that the developed system will actually achieve the stakeholders desired outcomes; Are you building the right product? What do you validate?

1078. What is the unit of forecast value?

4.4 Risk Audit: Microsoft Teams

1079. Do you record and file all audits?

1080. What does monitoring consist of?

1081. Do you have written and signed agreements/contracts in place for each paid staff member?

1082. Does your organization have a social media policy and procedure?

1083. Are risk assessments documented?

1084. Assessing risk with analytical procedures: do systemsthinking tools help auditors focus on diagnostic patterns?

1085. Mitigation -how can you avoid the risk?

1086. Are staff committed for the duration of the product?

1087. To what extent should analytical procedures be utilized in the risk-assessment process?

1088. Is an annual audit required and conducted of your financial records?

1089. Is all expenditure authorised through an identified process?

1090. Have you considered the health and safety of everyone in your organization and do you meet work health and safety regulations?

1091. What are the legal implications of not identifying a complete universe of business risks?

1092. Are corresponding safety and risk management policies posted for all to see?

1093. What responsibilities for quality, errors, and outcomes have been delegated to staff (or others) without adequate oversight?

1094. Are all programs planned and conducted according to recognized safety standards?

1095. Do end-users have realistic expectations?

1096. Extending the consideration on the halo effect, to what extent are auditors able to build skepticism in evidence review?

4.5 Contractor Status Report: Microsoft Teams

1097. Are there contractual transfer concerns?

1098. What are the minimum and optimal bandwidth requirements for the proposed soluiton?

1099. What process manages the contracts?

1100. Who can list a Microsoft Teams project as organization experience, your organization or a previous employee of your organization?

1101. How is risk transferred?

1102. What was the final actual cost?

1103. How does the proposed individual meet each requirement?

1104. What was the overall budget or estimated cost?

1105. What is the average response time for answering a support call?

1106. How long have you been using the services?

1107. What was the actual budget or estimated cost for your organizations services?

1108. If applicable; describe your standard schedule for new software version releases. Are new software version releases included in the standard maintenance plan?

1109. Describe how often regular updates are made to the proposed solution. Are corresponding regular updates included in the standard maintenance plan?

1110. What was the budget or estimated cost for your organizations services?

4.6 Formal Acceptance: Microsoft Teams

1111. Who would use it?

1112. What are the requirements against which to test, Who will execute?

1113. Was business value realized?

1114. Was the Microsoft Teams project work done on time, within budget, and according to specification?

1115. What function(s) does it fill or meet?

1116. Do you perform formal acceptance or burn-in tests?

1117. What is the Acceptance Management Process?

1118. Who supplies data?

1119. How well did the team follow the methodology?

1120. Was the client satisfied with the Microsoft Teams project results?

1121. Does it do what client said it would?

1122. Is formal acceptance of the Microsoft Teams project product documented and distributed?

1123. What features, practices, and processes proved

to be strengths or weaknesses?

1124. How does your team plan to obtain formal acceptance on your Microsoft Teams project?

1125. What lessons were learned about your Microsoft Teams project management methodology?

1126. Do you buy-in installation services?

1127. Was the Microsoft Teams project managed well?

1128. Do you buy pre-configured systems or build your own configuration?

1129. Does it do what Microsoft Teams project team said it would?

1130. Have all comments been addressed?

5.0 Closing Process Group: Microsoft Teams

1131. Are there funding or time constraints?

1132. Does the close educate others to improve performance?

1133. What were the actual outcomes?

1134. How dependent is the Microsoft Teams project on other Microsoft Teams projects or work efforts?

1135. Can the lesson learned be replicated?

1136. Were risks identified and mitigated?

1137. Did the delivered product meet the specified requirements and goals of the Microsoft Teams project?

1138. How well defined and documented were the Microsoft Teams project management processes you chose to use?

1139. What is the Microsoft Teams project name and date of completion?

1140. What is the Microsoft Teams project Management Process?

1141. What is the risk of failure to your organization?

1142. How well did the team follow the chosen processes?

1143. What is the overall risk of the Microsoft Teams project to your organization?

1144. What is the amount of funding and what Microsoft Teams project phases are funded?

1145. What can you do better next time, and what specific actions can you take to improve?

1146. Did the Microsoft Teams project team have enough people to execute the Microsoft Teams project plan?

1147. What level of risk does the proposed budget represent to the Microsoft Teams project?

5.1 Procurement Audit: Microsoft Teams

1148. Did your organization identify the full contract value and include options and provisions for renewals?

1149. Are buyers rotated so that they do not deal with the same vendors year in and year out?

1150. Were additional works strictly necessary for the completion of performance under the contract?

1151. Does the contract meet criteria of completeness and consistency?

1152. Is the purchasing department consulted on favorable purchasing opportunities, economic ordering quantities, and revision of purchasing specifications?

1153. Is the procurement process well organized?

1154. Is there a procedure to summarize bids and select a vendor?

1155. Are behaviour modification applied to change procurement of goods and services if procurement is not functioning properly?

1156. Were no charges billed to interested economic operators or the parties to the system?

1157. Is it clear which procurement procedure your organization has opted for?

1158. Were the documents received scrutinised for completion and adherence to stated conditions before the tenders were evaluated?

1159. Is there a policy on purchasing from users of organization products?

1160. Was a sufficient competitive environment created?

1161. Is there an approval policy in which the final cost of an order exceeds the amount originally estimated on the requisition or purchase order?

1162. Were all admitted tenderers invited to submit a tender for each specific contract?

1163. Is the minutes book kept current?

1164. Does your organization have an overall strategy and/or policy on public procurement, providing guidance for procuring entities?

1165. Do the internal control systems function appropriate?

1166. Are there procedures governing how sales and use tax will be handled (ordering in state versus ordering out of state)?

1167. Does your organization maintain a current file of vendors and vendor catalogues?

5.2 Contract Close-Out: Microsoft Teams

1168. Was the contract type appropriate?

1169. Parties: Authorized?

1170. Have all contracts been closed?

1171. Was the contract sufficiently clear so as not to result in numerous disputes and misunderstandings?

1172. What happens to the recipient of services?

1173. Why Outsource?

1174. How does it work?

1175. How/when used ?

1176. Have all contract records been included in the Microsoft Teams project archives?

1177. Have all contracts been completed?

1178. How is the contracting office notified of the automatic contract close-out?

1179. Was the contract complete without requiring numerous changes and revisions?

1180. Has each contract been audited to verify acceptance and delivery?

1181. Have all acceptance criteria been met prior to final payment to contractors?

1182. Change in attitude or behavior?

1183. Are the signers the authorized officials?

1184. Parties: who is involved?

1185. Change in circumstances?

1186. Change in knowledge?

1187. What is capture management?

5.3 Project or Phase Close-Out: Microsoft Teams

1188. What was the preferred delivery mechanism?

1189. What stakeholder group needs, expectations, and interests are being met by the Microsoft Teams project?

1190. Planned completion date?

1191. What were the goals and objectives of the communications strategy for the Microsoft Teams project?

1192. Who are the Microsoft Teams project stakeholders and what are roles and involvement?

1193. What process was planned for managing issues/ risks?

1194. What is the information level of detail required for each stakeholder?

1195. Who exerted influence that has positively affected or negatively impacted the Microsoft Teams project?

1196. What was learned?

1197. What benefits or impacts does the stakeholder group expect to obtain as a result of the Microsoft Teams project?

1198. What could be done to improve the process?

1199. Who controlled key decisions that were made?

1200. What information did each stakeholder need to contribute to the Microsoft Teams projects success?

1201. Is the lesson significant, valid, and applicable?

1202. What is in it for you?

1203. Did the delivered product meet the specified requirements and goals of the Microsoft Teams project?

1204. Who controlled the resources for the Microsoft Teams project?

1205. What are they?

1206. How often did each stakeholder need an update?

5.4 Lessons Learned: Microsoft Teams

1207. How accurately and timely was the Risk Management Log updated or reviewed?

1208. What skills did you need that were missing on this Microsoft Teams project?

1209. What is the proportion of in-house and contractor personnel authorized for the Microsoft Teams project?

1210. Overall, how effective were the efforts to prepare you and your organization for the impact of the product/service of the Microsoft Teams project?

1211. How well do you feel the executives supported this Microsoft Teams project?

1212. What solutions or recommendations can you offer that would have improved some aspect of the Microsoft Teams project?

1213. If you had to do this Microsoft Teams project again, what is the one thing that you would change (related to process, not to technical solutions)?

1214. Were quality procedures built into the Microsoft Teams project?

1215. How clear were you on your role in the Microsoft Teams project?

1216. How comprehensive was integration testing?

1217. What things mattered the most on this Microsoft Teams project?

1218. How effective were the techniques used to prepare you and your organization for the impact of the changes brought about by the product or service produced by the Microsoft Teams project?

1219. Was any formal risk assessment carried out at the start of the Microsoft Teams project, and was this followed up during the Microsoft Teams project?

1220. What would you like to see better documented about how to use existing processes on this type of Microsoft Teams project?

1221. What worked well or did not work well, either for this Microsoft Teams project or for the Microsoft Teams project team?

1222. Did the Microsoft Teams project improve the team members reputations, skills, personal development?

1223. How effective were Best Practices & Lessons Learned from prior Microsoft Teams projects utilized in this Microsoft Teams project?

1224. How did the estimated Microsoft Teams project Budget compare with the total actual expenditures?

1225. Does the lesson describe a function that would be done differently the next time?

1226. How effective was the architecture/system

design process?

Index

limited 11, 183
Linked 35, 216
listed 1, 180
listen 96, 111, 222
Litigation 190
located 218
logged 168, 212
logical 147, 158, 234
longer 78
long-term 77, 95, 109
looking 19, 169
losses 47
lowest 147, 156
machines 91
magnitude 72
mailbox 104
maintain 28, 47, 60, 76, 90, 116, 174, 247
maintained 161, 218, 235
makers 77, 122
making 21, 57, 65, 71, 89, 180, 183, 230
malware 93
manage 28, 31, 45, 59-60, 63, 71, 93, 97, 123, 130, 132, 138, 152, 154, 162, 165, 175, 180, 191, 195, 199, 221, 234
manageable 35
managed 7, 36, 81, 141, 168, 211, 243
management 1, 3-5, 9, 11-12, 18-19, 23, 33-34, 68-69, 90, 93, 101, 116-117, 121, 126, 129-132, 134, 140-141, 143, 148-149, 159, 161, 164-165, 167, 174-175, 179, 185-189, 192, 194-195, 199-200, 203-207, 209-210, 217, 230-231, 235-236, 239, 242-244, 249, 252
manager 7, 12, 20, 29, 32, 94, 140, 148, 199, 210
Managers 2, 120
manages 117, 123, 240
managing 2, 120, 125, 204, 250
Mandated 195-196
mandatory 213
manner 147, 169, 199, 211, 218, 234
mantle 92
mapped 35
market 25, 52, 224, 236
marketer 7
Marketing 101
markets 21
master 147

purpose   2, 11, 89, 140, 159, 172, 215, 225-226, 232-233
pushing   93
qualified   34, 140, 168
qualities   19
quality 1, 4-5, 11, 46, 52, 57, 61, 81, 83, 100, 118, 133, 167, 175,
177-180, 183-184, 199-200, 212, 217-218, 230, 239, 252
quantities   246
question   12-13, 17, 26, 41, 54, 64, 76, 88, 222
questions   7, 9, 12, 20, 62, 135, 164, 217, 229
quickly 12, 57, 61, 195
raised 141
rather 43, 99
rational   147
rationale   216
reached   23
reaching   114
reactivate   111
readings   77
realism 202
realistic   23, 97, 148, 239
Reality 224
realized   98, 242
really   7, 30, 43, 134, 181
real-time   57
reason 99, 104
reasonable   110, 199
reasonably   199
reasons   37, 133, 168, 177
recasts 170
receive   9-10, 32, 52, 206, 228
received   29, 96, 190, 201, 247
receivers   205
recently   11, 89
recipient   20, 248
recognised   69
recognize   2, 17-19, 22-23, 42, 69, 73
recognized   18-21, 57, 148, 162, 187, 224, 239
recognizes   20
recommend   89, 104, 141, 187
record 222, 238
recorded   168
recording   1, 222
records   58, 97, 146, 161, 203, 218, 235, 238, 248

remedies   41
remember   163
remove   71
remunerate   113
renewals   246
rephrased   11
replanning   146
replicated   244
Report 5-6, 53, 77, 132, 209, 220, 232, 240
reported   146, 177, 236
reporting   82, 189, 233, 235
reports 52, 85, 125, 130, 147-148, 170, 211, 234
repository   167, 185
represent   74, 173, 214, 245
reproduced   1
reputation   112
request   5, 62, 173-174, 211, 213-214
requested   1, 65, 174, 213
requests   117, 168, 211-212
require 29, 32, 46, 79, 158, 189, 203
required   20, 22, 24, 28-29, 31, 35-36, 47, 61, 66, 73-74, 81,
133, 135-136, 147, 150-152, 164, 168, 177, 185, 187, 189, 194-195,
203, 238, 250
requiring   125, 248
research   19, 25, 93, 126, 218
resemble   201
reserved   1, 52
reserves   235
reside 167, 201
resolution   61, 223
resolve 24, 220, 222
resolved   121, 189, 223
resource   3-4, 26, 32, 52, 104, 129, 143, 153, 158-160, 167,
185-186, 199, 204, 209, 223
resources   2, 9, 24, 33-34, 44, 68, 73, 79, 81-82, 100, 102, 104,
107, 136, 140, 150, 152, 157, 160, 167, 172, 199, 203, 205, 220,
233, 251
respect   1
respond   128
responded   13
responding   191
response   18, 25, 82-85, 201, 240
responses   113, 196

Lightning Source UK Ltd.
Milton Keynes UK
UKHW010819021019
350864UK00015B/1129/P